Praise for Peace, The Flip Side to Anger

"'Peace -The Flip Side to Anger' is the inspirational story of how Kornelia Stephanie overcame seemingly overwhelming challenges to turn her life around. Kornelia uses her own life experiences to show how we can heal ourselves and turn catastrophic events into triumphs of the spirit. The book gives us a roadmap with practical exercises to help us to find joy, peace and happiness in our own lives. There are life lessons in every chapter that are relevant to the challenges that we all face on our personal journeys. It's a fascinating and sometimes heart-rending story that leaves the reader with the tools and motivation to tackle their own demons and help others make this life wonderful!
~Tom Paulus

"This book is a profound message of remembering who we truly are. Kornelia has captured her journey and brilliantly shared it in a simple, practical way we can all relate to and apply in our own lives. She is a leader, way-shower, trail blazer in these most challenging and extraordinary times. After reading this book you will know you are not alone in your struggles and have access to a loving, kind hand to hold on your journey to greatness."
~Susan Glavin, *Author*

"'Peace the Flip Side to Anger', both the book, and Kornelia herself, are an inspiration. Through the author's own life experiences, infused with intuitive wisdom, Kornelia boldly and beautifully shines a light on the spectrum of emotions, allowing us all to identify and relate on a personal level. In an age where more people than ever are searching for answers, Kornelia shows us that joy, empowerment, and creativity can be our reality, and equips us with simple tools to make that happen."
~Robyn Pipkin, *Yoga Teacher, Life coach*

"This book has grown out of one woman's courageous and victorious journey from childhood misery to living fully in love and joy. Kornelia is a beacon of light to anyone dealing with the unresolved anger or depression that hides their authentic self, and her sessions and teachings are life changing. This book is like listening to her encourage you on your way. Her sincerity and love for humanity shine through on every page, and the workbook provides the individual steps that can take you from victim to victorious, from fear to love, and from anger to peace and happiness. Simply reading it is an immensely uplifting experience."

~Lori Thomas

PEACE
The Flip Side to Anger

Dear Mel

PEACE

♡

Liberty for all ♡

Thank you for all the
good you do and are
in the world.

I see you, I love you
Kornelia Stephanie

"Although anger can be destructive, it is also a potent tool. As long as anger is not expressed in destructive ways, getting to the root of our anger is our key for personal liberation."

Peace is an inside job
The key to change the
world is to change yourself

PEACE
The Flip Side to Anger

---

by Kornelia Stephanie

You came here to remember your true Divine Nature.

You are here to remember you are Infinite.

You came to experience yourself in the fullness of your Soul,

bringing Heaven to Earth.

Welcome to Paradise.

Kornelia Stephanie
2015

First Printing: 2015

ISBN 978-1-329-70522-7

Kornelia Stephanie
PO Box 119
La Conner, WA 98257
www.korneliaStephanie.com

Ordering Information:
Special discounts are available on quantity purchases by corporations, associations, educators, and others. For details, contact the publisher at the above listed address.

U.S. trade bookstores and wholesalers:
Please contact Kornelia Stephanie at the
email: info@korneliaStephanie.com

Dedication

This book is dedicated to all the children in the world, past, present, and future and my living angel, Robert Skeele.

Contents

Acknowledgements xiii

Preface xxi

Foreward xxv

Introduction xxvii

Part One - The Power of Emotions: Kornelia's Story

Chapter 1: *The Yard* 1

Chapter 2: *Peace is an Inside Job* 7

Chapter 3: *The Town Hall - From Victim to Victory* 15

Chapter 4: *The Trigger - Anger, The Flip Side to Peace* ... 23

Chapter 5: *From Anger to Peace* 31

Chapter 6: *The Addict* 43

Chapter 7: *Victims to Our Bodies* 51

Chapter 8: *Emotional Healing and Self-Regeneration* 59

Chapter 9: *From Prison to Freedom* 71

Chapter 10: *Heaven on Earth* 81

Part Two - The Peace Practice: Making Peace With Your Piece

87

The Peace Practice Intro 89

· What is Emotional Processing? 105

· Prepping for the Next 21 Days 115

The 21 Day Peace Practice 121

· Week One 121

· Week Two 149

· Week Three 177

Practical Tools: *A Toolbox for Everyday Living* 205
· Anger Management 101   209
· Kornelia's Emotional Processing Technique   219
· The Art of Releasing Fear   225
· The Script by Karol Truman   229
· Short Three-Step Peace Process   233

Part Three - The New Spiritual Human:
Change The World   235

Holistic References 237
· Drugged Into Oblivion: Nearly 60 Percent of All U.S.
  Adults Are On Prescription Drugs by Michael Snyder...   241
· With Newest Arrest, The NFL Should Impose A
  Unique Mandatory Anger Management Program...........   245
· Together We Are Changing the World 249
· Prayer of Saint Francis 255

About the Author 257

Acknowledgements

I took a village to birth this book, and it is possible because of my dear friends who supported me endlessly in all the stages of birthing this book and this message. This book was self-published and would not have been possible had it not been for them.

My dear friend **Kevin Doheny,** who has worked tirelessly with me, my undying gratitude to you, for all of your amazing skills as proof-reader, editor, videographer, and so much more. Thank you for your support in my life. Your contribution has been immense, and this book would not be without YOU and your wizard-ness and Jack of all Trades. I adore you.

My soul-sister and dear friend **Marianne Green,** the utmost gratitude to you for editing my book. Your devotion and love for my book and it's message made me fall in love again with my book. I deeply prize our friendship. Thank you for walking with me.

My very good friend **Larry Paille,** thank you for editing and your support in setting up the project right from the beginning. I am deeply honored and grateful for the detail and integrity you bring into all of your work. Thank you for always being there to help. My Love to you.

My soul-sister and dear friend **Wendy Binggeli,** thank you so much for proofreading my book, and being such a bright influence in my life, right from the beginning in offering your heart, time and love for my book. You continue to light my path. I am so grateful we are friends.

My dear friend and soul-sister **Lori Thomas**, thank you for editing and your continued support in my work. I am so honored by your friendship and the amazing gifts you bring.

My deep appreciation and gratitude to **Susan Skeele** for the final edit of this book. Your deep knowledge, helpful suggestions, along with your focus really helped bring this project to completion.

A special thank you to my best friend, **Robert Skeele** for giving me the title of the book that day at the post office. Thank you for the poetry you bring to my life.

Immense love and gratitude to my dear friend **Katy French**. Thank you for your gift of photography, taking my pictures, and capturing my true divine essence the way that you do. I deeply value and appreciate you.

My dearest wise goddess, **Nisha Bhatt**, thank you so much for designing the cover of my book and for making sure the formatting reached its optimal achievement in the printing of this book. Your commitment and joyful contribution has made this project a huge success. You are so very wise and a bright light in my heart.

Thanks to all the people in the background that also supported this book, and the launching of the peace campaign at Pike and Market in Seattle on September 6th, 2014. **Charleen Hess, Diane Light, Robyn Pipkin, Cecily Reading, Kerry Cody,** I am in such gratitude to all of you.

Thank you to all the peace ambassadors that promoted the book and the peace project with me on the 45-day Indiegogo campaign. I know that we made a huge contribution with being the peace we want to see in the world. At a time when there was so much chaos going on, we stayed strong in our center for Peace on Earth.

Thank you all so much for the money and the resources that have been offered through sponsorships and support to help this book land in the hands of people who cannot afford it.

I am deeply grateful to all of you who purchase the books and are inspired by the message: embodying peace within.

To my friends, YOU know who you are, thank you for standing by me as I found my way out of the jungle.

To my Momma, my best girl, I love you so much. Thank you for giving birth to me, and thank you for your love.

Let there be peace on earth and let it begin with Me.

From my heart to yours,
Kornelia

Imagine

Imagine a world where dreams come true.

Imagine all the people living life in peace.

Imagine a world where all the children are safe and fed.

Imagine a world where we all take responsibility for ourselves
and transmute our anger and pain into understanding,
setting ourselves free.

Imagine a world where we all live in freedom
as responsible leaders for our own lives.

Imagine a world where we all accept ourselves
and each other unconditionally.

Imagine a world where we all are in love with ourselves
and with all others.

Imagine a world where we all accept our greatness
and our divine birthright.

Imagine a world where Love is the law.

Imagine a world which is free of judgment,
free of struggle and free of pain.

Imagine a world where we the people
are radiating our true divine essence.

Imagine a world where we deeply feel joy and sorrow,
ecstasy and despair, knowing it nurtures us all equally.

Imagine a world which begins with each of us personally.

Imagine a world where Peace and Love are the choices made by all.

Imagine a world where this is already complete.

Imagine the endless possibilities.

Imagine a world where we now live as ONE.

Will you join us?

"You have the absolute ability to perceive and achieve world peace.
Accepting it begins inside of you. When you have made peace with
all that is out of harmony within, you will achieve inner peace.
Make peace with the opposing forces that are at war within yourself.
The world is your body, the mind is your Universe.
It is all inside of YOU."

~Kornelia Stephanie

Be Love and
Teach Peace.

My Philosophy

Peace is an inside job.

God, Source, Love is inside of YOU, not separate from You.

You have a choice to remember the truth of who you are.

Not taking ownership and responsibility for yourself
is the most damaging pattern.

The Point of Power is in the Present Moment.
That time is now. YOU only have NOW.

You are remembering your true Divine Nature.

Your true Divine Nature and your Essence are Love and JOY.

You are loved beyond measure, so adored that it will melt your
heart.

You are the creator of your world, conscious or unconscious.

You create with your thoughts, actions and feelings.

The Emotional Body is the most important area
to work with in healing your illnesses in the physical body.
Begin by examining your emotional suppressions.
Feel everything fully. Feeling it is healing it.

Meet your pain with fierce compassion and
use your consciousness to set yourself free.
Everything wants to be loved.

You have the power within to heal yourself

with love, compassion and understanding.
The most important act you can do today is to accept
and love yourself unconditionally, moment to moment.
This will ripple out to everyone.
Doubt is the biggest dream killer.

Your subconscious mind has been programmed
with limiting beliefs and negativity.

Open your heart's knowing to limitless possibilities.

The universe lives inside of you.
The outside world is but a reflection of within.

Release your past, release your anger, make room for Truth and
Love.

When you fully love yourself,
you have an intimate relationship with the Divine.
You bring all of yourself, the fullness of you, into your relationships.

I am that, I am.

To know me is to know yourself.

I love and adore YOU.

~Kornelia

Preface

What makes my book and my approach unique? I use anger as a tool for personal liberation. In a sense, my book is more than a book. It is a movement in the making, the beginning of the creation of a community of self-empowered individuals who are accepting 100% responsibility for themselves and their anger and thus are making huge peaceful contributions within themselves and within their communities. Anger is a powerful human raw emotion and all human beings have this emotion. But, most importantly, all of us have the ability to use our anger as creative fuel to make the necessary changes within ourselves. By taking our power back, we are in a position to support each other and make the changes that our collective evolution on this planet is calling us to make.

Why is anger important? It offers us the opportunity to release old suppressed feelings of victimhood, powerlessness and disease: to release them from our bodies. Anger is personal. We are the ones responsible for our liberation. No one else can do it for us. Only we can use our anger as a catalyst for empowerment. Whether male or female, we all have to deal with anger (emotion), and it is up to us to express our anger in a healthy way. It's part of our humanity. Healthy expression of anger occurs when the individual learns not to suppress anger but instead taps into his innate ability to deal with it by bringing it into the open. Our society and our conditioning has us buying into the belief that anger is bad and the only way to deal with it is to suppress it. The results of this have been devastating, causing many violent crimes against humanity. In his recent study of domestic violence in the NFL, Roger Groves, a Professor of Law at Florida Coastal School of Law, writes: "Anger is the root cause and common element of all these crimes against humanity, be it against a woman or child". I agree with Professor Groves statement, but I disagree that the solution is to control anger. Anger needs to be expressed in a healthy way, not controlled. In a report on gun violence in the schools, Michael Snyder points at that in recent years, nearly every school shooter was on antidepressant drugs which can cause people to behave in extremely irrational ways. It's time to take our organic nature back into our hands and teach one another how to process our emotions, how to express our anger constructively without drug dependency. (See both articles on page 247).

Anger is our tool for personal liberation. When an individual in angry, it is always his or her anger, and his or her loaded (gun.) The individual decides what to do with that energy, whether to load the gun and shoot back, or whether to use his fist and fight back, or to use his voice to yell and bully, or to project the anger out onto the other person or event - all of which are unhealthy ways to express anger.

The most important relationship you have is with yourself. The way you treat yourself is the way you treat others. Bullying in any form, for example, whether it comes from the little critical voice in your head, or from a bully in your environment making you feel powerless, should not be tolerated. If you feel powerless, that is a perfect opportunity for you to release from within your physical body old suppressed feelings of powerlessness. Work with this process, the results are life- changing. Tapping into your anger is emotional freedom, self-healing, freedom from being dependent on medications to numb up a feeling of depression, hopelessness or anxiety.

The Peace Practice in the second part of the book will assist you in collaborating with your higher-self in clearing and releasing all lower emotions of frustration and anger into freedom. You will transform your negative limiting beliefs into empowering beliefs that are more in alignment with who you are now after releasing your anger. Integrating your shadow, you are becoming your own healer.

If you follow the Peace Practice, you will learn to accept and welcome responsibility without resentment or shame, release anger creatively, gain ability to stay in a peaceful, centered place while living in a state of joy, having expressed anger in ways that promote physical and mental well being.

"Anger is an acid that can do more harm to the vessel in which it is stored than to anything on which it is poured."

-Mark Twain

Foreward

When I was a little girl under the age of 10, I used to go to bed and cry myself to sleep at night. I would pray to God not to give me children until I would know what to do with them. I never wanted another child to feel what I was feeling, and my whole life has been about healing the inner child within me. This is still a work in progress today. Even though I desperately wanted and needed to be needed and loved, I put my need and want to have a child aside to really tend to my own healing, my own nurturing of my wounded child within.

I never had children, yet the work I do and have done with my clients and many others is about the healing of the inner child within. The birth of this book is inspired by my desire to speak out for all the children in the world who deserve to live in peace and harmony.

In the launching of an Indiegogo Peace Campaign I took a strong public stance along with the many others who support me in my mission to educate and bring about awareness that Peace is an inside job. Peace really begins with each of us taking responsibility for our own thoughts, emotions and actions.

I want World Peace! As I am speaking for the children; I need to share what I know works. This book is my personal story. My experiences are examples of 'moving beyond the story' to educate and create awareness about taking responsibility through a non-violence approach. We see many angry people projecting their emotions/

anger out into the world, and onto each other. We see it right here at home in our country, our communities, our places of work, as well as in our personal relationships. There are many people who feel remorseful when they get angry. I want to bring light to the idea that it is good for them to get in touch with their anger, some of which has been suppressed for a long time. In this book, *Peace, the Flip Side to Anger*, I share my approach so everyone can experience these shifts.

You know how a lot of times we look back at our life and say: "I wish I had known then what I know now?" I wish someone had told me about emotions, anger, and feelings – and what to do with them. I want to tell this to as many people as possible. There are many ways we can practice peace: yoga, meditation, positive thinking, and conscious breathing, for example. But the one key component is getting to the root of our anger and accepting responsibility for it.

I am writing this book to help others who may be able to see themselves in my story.

Sincerely from my heart,
Kornelia

Introduction

I believe I chose to be here. I chose my parents, co-created my script with the sole purpose of remembering my connection with Source. I needed to release, heal, and transmute back into Divine Love everything which was/is not love.

We came here to co-create a new world, and we have all we need inside ourselves to graduate from the Earth class as Masters.

I don't know many people who had happy childhoods. I have met a few of these people along my journey, but I was not one of them. From the time I was a little girl I was very awake to the fact that I was different. My life and my childhood did not look the same as my friends, or others in my community. I always felt a cloud of shame hanging over me.

I was born and raised in Germany. My mother and father (both alcoholics) separated and divorced before I was three and my mom had the job of providing for three children on her own. I remember early on that dirty and shameful feeling because my childhood was anything but stable. In fact, it was completely dysfunctional. The foundation on which I grew up was unstable. This feeling was something that followed me my entire life, and I always tried to cover it up.

My mother told me - a very young child - that I needed to help her and that it was my job to support her. From the very beginning, I learned to never acknowledge myself. I put my own needs aside so that I could be there for my family.

Shortly after my mother and my father divorced, I got really, really sick with a lung infection and was in the hospital for about a month. I realize this was my body's way of not being able to accept and deal with the grief, feeling so hurt where love was concerned. My father being absent and my mother having to work all the time, there was nobody there to nurture me. I almost died (this was my first possible exit point to leave my body).

I remember being in the hospital. When I was admitted, I was completely starved for love and nurturing, and I recall being loved and nurtured back to health by the nurses. I did not have much education, as we were always moving and my energy was preoccupied with other things. Here again, I noticed that I did not fit in and was different from the other kids.

I also witnessed my mom taking a lot of abuse. She was trying to find a man who would help her raise her children, yet she kept attracting the wrong men. One time she was beaten so badly that she could not go to work for over a month. I had to stay home from school to take care of her.

I remember the morning I walked into her bedroom when she had a sheet over her head. I thought she was dead. I pulled the sheet back, and I did not recognize her. Her boyfriend had taken her to the woods, tied her up to a tree and beaten the living shit out of her.

Yet there were dear memories. I would spend a lot of time alone, and when I got home from school, it was my job to clean the house from top to bottom. This was such a huge job that I started talking to my angels, and I would have them help me clean the house. There was a whole group of them and they all had names. I would teach them how to clean. It just seemed to make it easier for me to have them help me.

The older I got, the more painful the feeling of rebellion arose in me. I saw my mom drinking with greater frequency, and she was always crying. During those nights I would go to bed and cry and beg

God: "Please dear God, do not give me children until I know what to do with them. I do not want any child to experience this kind of pain that I am feeling."

We moved to America when I was 15. Mom married my new stepfather, a military African-American man who was very disciplined. He provided a structure for my family to heal. I, though, was showing signs of rebellion in a big way. The sexual abuse that I had experienced, and the witnessing of my Mom having been beaten by her boyfriends, left me internally enraged. Even though I was very grateful to my stepfather, I had some huge wounds which they did not know how to handle. Shortly thereafter, I ran away from home, and for the next 11 years, I became very successful in my business endeavors. Then, before age 30, I quickly began to self-destruct. Because I did not know how to hold, celebrate or manage my success, I sabotaged it all. Then, and only then, was this painful gift of self-destruction realized. Failure was the gift. It prepared me to begin peeling the onion off low self-worth, low self-esteem, one layer at a time. Looking back today I can see how my inner saboteur was calling to be loved free - and what a gift that has been.

I know the universe lives inside of me. I came into this life to embody my freedom, to experience and express the fullness of the truth of who I am. I came into this life to remember myself and set myself free. I had to do it for myself.

I came into this life to embody my true divine blueprint, to create my life on a foundation that is rooted in love, peace, and prosperity, and to birth a new consciousness, co-creating Paradise right here on Earth.

The Setup Was Brilliant

The script: return to love and peace, freedom, unconditional love, self-acceptance, and create Paradise on Earth.

The challenge: overcome self-hatred, lack of consciousness, slavery, addictions, victim consciousness, and separation from Source with a big label of NOT WORTHY on the back and the front of this girl.

The dream: to release myself from prison, the inner prison being mirrored for me by the outside world. The church told me someone was coming. I waited and waited a long time, 30 years or so. When I realized nobody was coming, then I had to do it myself. It was up to me if and when I wanted to be free.

It took me 20 years to free myself, two decades to undue all the programming and to find my own inner authority. I had been taught so many ideas and had such negative programming; I began to question everything: my beliefs, my ideas, my assumptions, and my own inner truth. I discovered that what had so angered me were my feelings of powerlessness beneath all that rage. In releasing those feelings, I accessed the truth of my being.

Releasing Myself From Prison

I used my body, which I think of as my alchemical tool, to release myself from prison. This is what this book is about.

There are rules and laws here in this 'prison' (in the third dimension) that are about control and manipulation. The game being played is not the truth, and it is up to each of us to decode the mystery and discover the magic. We become our own judge, our own authority, our own parole board - taking responsibility for ourselves, setting ourselves free.

I notice there are many other prisoners here who also have life sentences. Many of them are asleep. They get to choose if and when they want to be free. It is a universal law. We all have free will. These 'inmates' too get to choose if they want to leave their inner prison and co-create Paradise here on Earth. Many prisoners have been conditioned in such a way that they are afraid of their own freedom. They do not know what to do with it. They would much rather stay in their familiar comfort zone, being told what to do and when to do it, living from a place of limitation and ration. But, again, we all have to choose for ourselves. That is the beauty of being here. We all have free will. We all get to choose.

Freedom has to be felt and experienced inside the body, and for that to occur, there has to be room. If the body still has the trauma, pain, lies and limitations stored inside (in the DNA of every cell), we can't feel freedom. Freedom and the feeling of imprisonment can't occupy the same space. The key is to make room, and the way we make room is by letting go. We have to let go of everything that is no longer of value or in alignment with our freedom.

I was released from my inner prison on April 14th, 2014, after a long conscious path. I remember that day. I was so overwhelmed by the freedom that I was feeling inside, that I could not even appreciate it to the fullest. I am still in awe. I knew this would take some time to integrate and get used to, and I am still getting used to it. Can you imagine what it feels like for me to live my life now as a free being, after being 'imprisoned' the greater part of it? It takes a while to get used to life after abuse.

My Life Has Been My Education
I Learn Through My Experiences

My life is my art and my past has been my schooling. I have just now graduated with honors after 47 years of life education. I have a Master's Degree in self-healing, physical, mental and emotional well-being, plus a master's degree in human relations, self-love, leadership and responsibility, as well as a universal master's degree in

spirituality, embodying unconditional love and higher consciousness. All this has trained me to be a master in experiential teaching.

I know this sounds like I am bragging, and you know what? I am! I
am so very proud of how far I have come.

I have a direct relationship with my Source

I have deeply studied relationships, how I relate to life, and all things
that are part of this glorious unfolding. I have cultivated an intimate
love relationship with my Source. I do not look outside of myself
for answers or approval. This has been hard, hard work. My journey
has been to really get to know myself and to come to have 100% acceptance of myself. I absolutely know what a gift that is to myself,
and to the collective.

All my life, I was always looking for someone to give me the magic
pill. I was always trying to fit in, to fit myself into the mold, to prove
that I could do it, to prove that I was lovable, to prove that I was deserving. I worked really hard to be super accommodating, to put others before myself, to prove and prove and prove that I was worthy,
always looking for someone to accept me. It never worked. We are
not meant to find that approval and acceptance from others. Our approval and acceptance has to come from within. When we love and
accept ourselves, we bring that love and acceptance into the world
by being the example. Gandhi said: "Be the change that you wish to
see in the world." I say: "Be the love that you wish to see in the world,
be the peace that you wish to see in the world, and and when you do,
you will be emitting a frequency of love and peace that will change
the world." We are not meant to fit into the old world, we are meant
to create a new one, and the time for doing so is now.

The Warrior in me knew that, first and foremost on the agenda, I
needed to undo all of the old negative programming inside of myself, and heal my painful emotional core wounds. I needed to stop
giving my power away to people, situations and events. To love my-

self whole and free was no easy task for someone who harbored self-hatred at the core. The hardest part for me was to take 100% responsibility for everything that showed up in my life, rather than blame others. Taking responsibility leaves everyone else off the hook. I have even had people I love leave my life, and have had to be OK with that in order to stay true to my own personal integrity. As I am taking quantum leaps on the evolutionary fast track, I am not taking any prisoners or victims with me. I have to be ok with that in order to stay true to my own personal integrity.

The purpose of this book is to share with you how I have healed my life, and to show you how you can do it, too. You don't need thousands of dollars to do it. You have everything you need right now to begin.

Peace is one of the highest vibrations you can reside in, being in harmony with your Spirit, being and feeling totally open and relaxed to receive and experience the many states of being that your body loves;, feeling tranquil, calm and centered. Being at peace is being ageless, timeless, and unlimited. When you are at peace, you are experiencing perfection in freedom and oneness.

"You have the absolute ability to perceive and achieve world peace.
Accepting it begins inside of you. When you have made peace with
all that is out of harmony within, you will achieve inner peace.
Make peace with the opposing forces that are at war within yourself.
The world is your body, the mind is your Universe.
It is all inside of YOU."

~Kornelia Stephanie

Be Love and Teach Peace.

Part One

The Power of Emotions:
Kornelia's Story

"If you want to awaken all of Humanity
then awaken all of yourself.
If you want to illuminate the
suffering in the world,
then illuminate all that darkness
and negativity within yourself.
Truly the greatest gift you have to give
is that of your own transformation."

~Lao Tzu

Chapter 1

The Yard

We are in an expansive cycle. We are learning the spiral dance that goes along with the evolution of expanding and releasing. This growth involves letting go. It feels like we are constantly being shown how to align with our truth. Living on the leading edge seems to be the norm. What norm? Nothing is normal.

We are moving up the spiral of our life's cycle, from the theme of evolving by experiencing all that we are not, to moving into the cycle of remembering and experiencing all that we are.

At our feet is a world and a field of unlimited potential and unlimited possibilities. I call us the 'letting go tribe'. We are letting go of everything, as everything is changing and nothing will ever be the same again. I don't know if you can tell, but we actually have no control over the evolution that is taking place; it is happening and change is constant. We can, however, make it easier on ourselves by releasing the resistance, and embracing the changes. We are the pioneers, creating a new way of being and living. The old way has lost its juice: it is boring. Click through the channels on the TV and see how bored we are. We are ready for the new. We are ready for love, prosperity, peace, creativity, acceptance, joy, magic, miracles, intimacy, community, and connection. We are ready to be free, and we want our Freedom.

Yet, at the same time, there is a lot of war and fighting on this planet. Strife and wars have been going on for eons, only now things are heating up faster.

We Are Being Asked to Take
Responsibility for Our Actions

We are being called to stop blaming and judging each other, to stop perpetuating separation and illusion. We are being asked to release all that is not in alignment with our truth, both individually and collectively. From one day to the next we don't know what innocent person or bystander might be killed, because someone walks out and starts shooting from anger. Who is pointing the finger at whom, projecting onto another? You never know when somebody is going to explode, or 'go postal', killing innocent people. It is such crazy madness to witness. The children who look to us have no voice; shuffled around, killed, while adults are screaming at each other. The elderly are ignored. The ones who are fighting are avoiding taking responsibility. Everybody is pushing each other's buttons, everywhere egos are flying out of control. The media, through their reporting, spread the toxin further, triggering people even more.

The contrasts on the world stage are a perfect opportunity for us to clear our bodies of the energies with which we are no longer in alignment. Only then can we start discovering what is true for ourselves.

Peace is the hot topic right now. There are many people experiencing some very difficult times. They have had enough and they want change, they want the madness to stop (or so they say). They want peace... but do they really? They keep looking to our leaders or others to fix everything for them, and can't understand why these 'leaders' don't do anything. Why is nothing changing in their environment? The secret is: Peace is an inside job.

Breaking Out of Prison

The way I see the world: we are breaking out of prison. We are claiming our freedom so we can experience our divine birthright. We are living in this giant prison that we no longer need. We are done playing the game of being prisoners. We are claiming our freedom, one heart at a time.

We have many different groups in our 'prison yard'. We have different races, elders, indigenous folk, religious groups, corporate giants. We have world leaders and we have people who know how to get things done. We have the undercover, we have the Illuminati, the Saints, the rich, the poor, the sick, the healthy, the visible and the invisible friends. We have them all. We have lines and we have the borders of where we can cross or where we cannot. It is crazy, fun, madness.

All these people, groups and gangs are fighting to uphold their images. The corporate people are trying to stay professional and are very uptight and stressed out. Before they came to planet Earth these tribes made many vows and pacts. All was prearranged so that healing could later begin. Now they are angry because they know that they don't agree with those vows anymore. They don't agree with the vow of poverty which their religion has forced upon them. They don't agree to being a slave to society. They don't agree with the bullshit. They want the suffering to stop, but they don't know how.

We will show them. It's not done by force, or manipulation, or control, or power over each other. It is done through self-empowered leadership, self-responsibility, respect and honor for one's self and for each other. We are our own judges, as well as our own authorities.

There are some people who have figured out how to get out of prison and they have created a pathway for others. They have stretched their minds and opened their hearts. They have faced the darkness within and now have become a bridge for others. The bridge is invisible to the naked eye, yet the bridge has all the colors of the most amazing rainbow you have ever seen. The grounded, awakened-ones are helping others who are ready to claim their freedom. They have been quietly working in the background, and are the ones who will support the others when they wake up. They have been there in full support, holding the space for all to come, holding the space for one another, holding the space until each and every one can hold it themselves.

The plan is to go from the 'yard' to the 'playground', but that takes some work. It takes courage, commitment, practice, as well as some quiet, deep inner work. You have to be willing to go deep within yourself. Be aware that the ego will be sitting on your shoulder screaming in your ear, like a three year old having a tantrum, the ego being scared, screaming: "What about me"?

Compassion

This work is not easy and can be painful. What I can tell you is that the pain will pass like a bad summer storm that came in the night. In the morning the sun will rise again, greeting you with a smile. Have compassion for yourself, the greatest gift you can offer to your awakening.

The awakened ones are understanding and have compassion. They, too, used to be inmates. Knowing what it takes, they have cleared the path and are holding the space with deep love and compassion for the rest of us. They know we are all in this together.

The beauty is that, regardless of the things that seem to divide us here, we are all united in truth. We really all want the same things, but don't know how to communicate when there is so much anger and violence within and without.

We all have hearts and our nature is love. We all have rage, we all have feelings, we all have bodies, we all want to live doing what we love with the people we love, eating good food, enjoying abundance for all. We want to be free, living joyfully on the most beautiful planet which has so much to teach us, so much to communicate, and so much beauty for us to experience. All who are ready to come will have to make a few stops along the way to release the baggage which is too heavy to take on the journey over the rainbow bridge and onto the playground.

We Are the Ones We Have Been Waiting For

All are welcome, regardless of race, gender, color, spiritual beliefs, religion, rich or poor, young or old. We are all in this together, we are all kin, we are all masters, we all have what it takes.

Now it is time to choose. Let us raise our consciousness and get busy. We have children to guide. We have a planet to create. The world is at our fingertips.

"Come to the edge, he said.

We are afraid, they said.

Come to the edge, he said.

They came to the edge,

He pushed them and they flew.

Come to the edge, Life said.

They said: We are afraid.

Come to the edge, Life said.

They came. It pushed them...

And they flew."

~Guilliame Apollinaire

Chapter 2

---⋙⋘---

Peace is an Inside Job

I f all people took responsibility for their own anger, thoughts, actions and feelings, we would have Peace, World Peace, instantly. Peace begins within. Peace is an inside job.

Anger / Violence

Take a look at all the anger (fire) that is being expressed right now: in your household, relationships, your work environment, around the world. So many people are feeling angry inside their bodies about the world in which we live. People point their fingers, take on the victim role, and do not accept responsibility for their own parts.

Deeply rooted, unacknowledged anger is the number one cause for war. The violence that is happening could end if people knew how to release their suppressed underlying emotions, anger. The violence could end if people stopped blaming or projecting onto other people and situations.

Violence does not happen by itself. Violence happens by one person, like a gunman walking into a church or any other building, killing innocent people out of rage.

Suppressed Emotions

Who knows how long you have been holding onto your suppressed emotions. The body, our beautiful earthly temple, holds onto so much. Any instances where you have to keep quiet and not say anything, out of fear, you suppress the energy in the body: fear of not being accepted, not fitting in, being ridiculed, possibly losing your job, maybe even getting killed if you are in a violent domestic relationship.

Anger does not need to be expressed in a violent way or be suppressed by numbing with addiction or distraction. The results of numbing are physical abuse, depression and sabotage of the body.

Although anger can be destructive, it is also a potent tool. Getting to the root of our anger is our key to personal liberation.

In the midst of all of this turmoil,
I pray that if I can only manage the terrorism of my own mind,
that will be enough.
~Janet Bray Attwood

The Solution

The solution is really very simple. It comes down to education: creating awareness about the energy within our bodies that needs to move. The solution lies in educating individuals how to move that energy in a conscious, responsible way.

Perhaps, in the past, wanting to keep the peace, you ignored your feelings and did not say anything. Now, in becoming conscious, when you get triggered, YOU GET ANGRY. By expressing your feelings you are releasing the stuck energy out of your physical body, and amazing liberation takes place. The process is simple: the old, stuck energy which has laid dormant in the body, stored in the DNA within the cells, begins to move. Having released the stuck energy, you are now more aligned with your truth. The body feels lighter, more vital, and you begin to feel more at peace.

Anger is energy in motion (emotion), and this energy needs to move. When energy/emotion gets expressed, it moves; energy is fluid. When energy/emotion gets suppressed, it causes stress in the body and can cause physical pain and serious illness. Think about when you are angry. How do you hold that energy in your body? Where do you hold it? Ask yourself: "Where am I feeling this in my body?" When you feel the negative emotions, all of them, the energy is released. This is the most natural, organic process of healing.

Love Your Anger

I want you to look at anger in a new way. I want to show you that getting angry is an opportunity to release old energy, an opportunity to make space in your body, an opportunity to claim freedom. Can you, instead of feeling bad when you get angry or judging yourself, or projecting the anger onto the other person, embrace the experience, knowing that it is happening so that you can release old programming and density out of your physical body? The incident which has triggered you is happening for you, not to you. This is the perfect opportunity to surrender and release the victim and its story. You belong to the 'letting go tribe'.

Victimhood

Albert Einstein said, "We can't solve the problem from the same consciousness that created it." If you keep the madness going by projecting the anger out (the same as we have always done), then don't be surprised when you keep getting the same results. To get different results, you have to be the catalyst for the change to take place, and use your body as a tool; as a releasing tool.

There are so many things that people are angry about, stemming from old paradigms, beliefs imprinted on us by our parents, our churches, our school system, our government. Later we discover that we are not in alignment with those beliefs. Anybody would be pissed off. People have a right to be angry. It's energy, it's fuel, it's part of how we express ourselves as humans. Then there is the Illuminati: we have been severely lied to and programmed. In the big picture, the memory held in the body is now getting activated by the trigger so that we can release what is no longer true.

The anger that you are feeling is your anger, your pain, your sadness - not anybody else's. What is underneath the anger is resentment, suppression, pain, frustration, powerlessness, victimhood. Nobody put it there. It is there because you have been holding onto it. Remind yourself continuously, when are you triggered, that you are purging, purifying and letting go. If you did not have a cellular memory in your body of a past wound, you would not be reacting.

The trigger gives us the opportunity to claim our power and release the victim energy. We are NOT victims. We choose to claim our power and approach the situation from a place of empowerment, compassion and leadership.

Every event is basically neutral. We are NOT victims.

Stepping back, can we offer acceptance, space and love to ourselves? Can we offer acceptance, space and love to each other, instead of judging one another and blaming one another?

One Flew Over the Cuckoo's Nest

I remember twenty years ago how angry I was inside. I was literally screaming that the world needs to change. "People need to do something." When I finally checked myself into a hospital, the doctors and nurses didn't know what to do with me, or my anger. So, they gave me high doses of medication like Lithium and Haldol to suppress me and shut me up. A side effect of the medications is constipation. I became so constipated, as well as suppressed, that they had to give me suppositories and enemas. You know what it's like to be constipated. I was holding on for dear life. I was not in a safe nurturing environment because I was being suppressed with medication and my body responded by holding on. I was not releasing anything. I was frozen, all clogged up and suppressed. When I finally realized what was happening to me, I stopped taking the medication they were giving me. I just pretended to take it. I would ask my doctor if he would sign the release papers and he said no, that I was not ready. I came to the conclusion that it was a financial matter, as my insurance was paying for my hospital stay. It was benefiting the hospital for me to stay and keep me medicated, and suppressed.

After 2 weeks, and as divine timing would have it, through my awareness of what was going on there, I was totally supported to shift my reality. One day I was in the hallway and a Patient Rights Activist started talking to me. After telling him what was going on, within the next 2 hours I had a hearing with a judge and lawyers, and was released from the hospital, overriding my doctor's authority.

This situation gifted me the opportunity to claim my authority and to claim my power back. With a little help from my Divine Team, I was released.

Had it not been for this Patient Rights Activist (one of God's angels and the many helpers we all have available at all times), I don't know what would have happened. Make no mistake, I had to choose which way to go. I had to play my part. I wonder how many people are in hospitals or prisons who don't belong there. This is one of the reasons why this work is so important to me.

I needed a space to release the pain, anger, and energy that I was feeling inside: without medication. I knew how to suppress myself, having gone through my own addictions. I knew how to keep the lid on my fire, my anger, for a long time. I knew how to keep myself numb and suppressed because feeling the feelings and feeling the pain, which I had held onto through many years of drug abuse, would be too overwhelming, too much to take.

My hospital experience was like One Flew Over the Cuckoo's Nest. When I was released, I realized that I was all alone. They, the world, did not know what to do, kind of like my parents not knowing what to do with me.

This example would be a case study for people who have experienced severe trauma in their lives, the kind of people who might be capable of a violent act, not because they are doomed, labeled, or bad at the core, but because they need a space to land, a space to be seen, heard, witnessed, understood, and validated. Offering this space to someone is offering peace. Offering this space to myself was my job.

Around that same time, I heard the statement that we choose our parents. Hearing this rang so true to me that I got goose bumps all over my body. It was then that a light bulb went off! I realized that I could no longer blame my mother anymore for my life or what was happening to me, as all had been my choice: I chose her, I chose my absent father, I chose my life to clear and heal myself. It's my responsibility, nobody else's. After being in the hospital, I did not want them to be responsible for me because their way did not work. This experience scared the crap out of me, but it also empowered me, as it put the focus on me, not on them. I had checked myself into the hospital because I wanted the doctors to do something about my pain and anger. In the end, I left the hospital with more anger than I came in with. They did what they knew how to do: prescribe medication and apply a pressure band-aid on top.

"Do you want real peace?
Peace has never come
from dropping bombs.
Real peace comes from
enlightenment and education
to behave in a more
divine manner."

~Carlos Santana

Chapter 3

∾०ᢗᢦᢦᢒ०ᢗ

The Town Hall - From Victim to Victory

The layers of anger, suppression, powerlessness, and the letting go of the victim energy are showing up for all of us right now. Are we willing to see it? Are we willing to release, transmute, transcend our victimhood and claim our power?

Powerlessness is what the real anger is all about. We are angry, tired of being afraid and being bullied. By releasing victim consciousness from the body, we create a different experience for ourselves and each other. Think about peeling layers of an onion. Imagine that each layer being removed represents unspoken suppression. These layers could be all the times in our lives when we gave our power away to another person, situation or event. In the end, it is our fire that is calling us: "Get conscious with me! Get intimate with me! Use me as the fuel to burn away all that is not the truth!"

When Is It Going to Stop?
Role Models and Domestic Violence

I clearly see that educating people about their anger will produce amazing results.

Think about the many places where violence is expressed: in the workplace, at home, in relationships. Now, think about creating an awareness that shows people how to work with anger. Domestic violence and expressions of anger, which are highlighted in the news constantly, are good examples. Take a look at the NFL. I would love to get my foot in the door to coach and educate these 'role models' on what to do with their anger. Our youth looks up to them. It is a privilege to play professional sports and with that comes a great responsibility to 'model' integrity.

There is a lot of focus on domestic violence now. This is not acceptable behavior anymore. And, it's not just the men, it's also the women. There was recently the incident with the US women's national soccer team: Hope Solo, an American soccer goalkeeper and a two time Olympic Gold Medalist, was charged with domestic violence.

Jillian Loydan, a US Soccer goalkeeper, retires from professional soccer claiming we must take a stand on abuse. Jillian broke the silence about her sister, Britton Loyden, who lost her life as a victim of domestic violence.

There are countless stories like this, many occurring right next door to us. We have the responsibility to educate and create awareness about what to do with the anger inside of ourselves, and how not to project it out onto other human beings. I clearly see that educating people about their anger will produce amazing results.

Depression

Depression is anger turned inward. Then there is a silent killer underneath: anger suppressed in the body that shows up as depression. How many suicides have happened this year alone? Some very famous souls and people we love took their lives as the energy was so depressed - suppressed - that they saw no way out.

Suicide can be prevented by bringing the energy that is depressed up from that very low place and moving it into the power center. Get them good and 'pissed off' and have them use that fuel to make positive changes in their lives. When people are depressed, rather than giving them medication, find out what is underneath that depression that needs to be acknowledged. Get them off the couch. Get their stuck energy moving. Educating people about how to release anger will produce empowering results.

The results will be phenomenal. Reducing crime, domestic violence, and murder will save the taxpayers money because it will reduce the need for prisons, as well as mental health facilities. It will offer those who are hurting the opportunity for so much more freedom. Let us use the money saved to create educational programs that raise awareness about helping neighbors, communities and schools to create safe environments in which people can thrive.

Creating With the Universe

'The Universe' is always communicating with us, reflecting back to us what we are creating. Through our perception we can heal ourselves through our experience, if we are open to see it. We can experience miracles, magic, and synchronicities right here all the time. What I have come to learn is that whatever I am working on or whatever I am trying to manifest creates and draws to me the right people and situations.

Contrast

When I myself am not 100% in alignment with the energy of what I desire, I experience contrast. This appears in the form of energies that are not congruent with my 'desires'. A negative charge around what I am experiencing is my first clue to take a look at what the underlying anger is really about. To finally arrive at truth and authenticity, what must I burn away? The contrast is important so that I can become conscious and consequently clear and purify my own energies within my body.

For example, the writing of this book took on a life of it's own. For months I had been searching and asking Source: "What is the #1 cause for war?" Anger! The answer always comes through our own experience, that is how we learn.

What is being reflected to me by the outside world? What is happening within me that I need to unify in myself completely in order to be at peace? In processing the wounds of the entire universe through my physical body, applying the above process and 'The Emotional Processing Technique', I know this work so deeply. Once I begin working with something, I own it fully, I go all in, I put my heart, soul and body into the experience. The Universe is my partner, setting up the perfect scenes in a movie where I get to be the starring actor, fully supported by my divine team. All the perfect supporting actors can show up to help me create my experience. It will either match my desire, or it will show me where I have work to do.

Seeking Peace on Earth

My deepest desire is Peace on Earth. I am a warrior at heart, a woman, who says: "Enough. Enough for me and for all life on this planet." I began talking to Source daily, listening, looking at what the world was reflecting back to me. I witnessed what people were discussing, what was happening to them, what they were tired of, and what was happening in their worlds. I saw anger being projected back and forth. I recognized the victim consciousness underlying the feelings of powerlessness.

Wherever in my life, inside myself, I was still feeling the energy of the victim, the feelings of powerlessness came up for release. For example, I wanted to organize a peace festival, gathering people in the community to connect with each other, to spread love and joy, to celebrate peace with i.e. music, art and food.

I talked to the mayor about a location, here in my home town, to create the peace festival, asking him about land, space, a park where we could hold this event. The mayor said he does not have the 'power' (key word here) to help me. I would need to go to the city council, tell them my idea, and then the city council would make the decision. I felt deflated by his response. He may not have the power, but honey, if you believe in the cause and you like what I am talking about, then you have a voice, and you are the mayor, and in my opinion, that's enough.

So I went to the town hall. Walking in, I saw directly in front of me a man who had projected vast amounts of anger onto me 18 months ago. He and I had been working for the same company. During that incident, he pointed his finger at me, just two inches from my nose, while he shouted names at me. When I reported this unacceptable incident to the business owner, she, too, felt powerless to address the situation. I ended up quitting my job. He still works there.

It was a perfect setup: when seeing this person at the town hall, I noticed my body wanting to turn around and walk out. There I was at the town hall to talk to the city officials about a space for my Peace Festival, and a perpetrator was standing in front of me. I felt like running and hiding. I heard an inner voice say: "Stay, you got this, don't run, walk up to the counter and stand up for what you believe in." He never saw me!

After getting back to my car, I thought about the healing that had just taken place. For me, it was not about the perpetrator, but about my releasing my fear, releasing my victim consciousness, about my claiming my own power.

This leads me to think even more about all the children who are at our mercy. I am a voice for them. I am standing up for the child in me, and I am standing up for all the children around the world.

When I got home that afternoon I had another surprise waiting for me. Three days earlier I had rented a room in my house to a man who was now acting like Mad Dad, a time bomb if you will. Over the next several days he severely triggered me, and I had the opportunity to release even more suppressed anger. My home had gone from being a peaceful, harmonious sanctuary, where my other room-mate and I felt safe and relaxed, to a home where we felt like we had to tiptoe around Mad Dad, who at any moment was going to go off on us. Who knew what this guy might be capable of. I asked him to move out and he said: "YOU can't make me".

All kinds of rage, fire and anger arose in me.

Another perfect setup! My inner bullet went off. I reflected on what was happening within myself, my feelings around this man being in my home. What a gift this experience was bringing me! It also made me realize that the energy of intimidation is the energy that every woman, man, and child feels when they are being bullied. This is the war, and it is in my house, and Momma is saying enough is enough. I felt like a lioness in her cage prancing back and forth, being trained to be gentle, to come out and meet the humans for the first time.

"What pisses me off has nothing to do with you. So don't take it personally that you are the catalyst for activating my anger, creating the opportunity for me to use that fire and responsibly create a different reality. It's my anger, my rage, my fuel and my freedom. It has nothing to do with you, YOU get to be you, all of you, without question, without the need that you need to change. What you do or do not do, has nothing to do with me."

~Kornelia Stephanie

Chapter 4

─────◦◦⌒◦◦─────

The Trigger - Anger, the Flip Side to Peace

We don't fight war with fighting back. We don't fight war with war. When I was being triggered and feeling bullied in my own home, I could have fought back. Instead, I released the feelings of powerlessness within me and then claimed my power by taking bold action. I knew this bully was hurting and I knew this bully was wounded and was taking it out on me. I am not a victim here. I first had to release my fear of him taking power over me, and then coming back to him meeting him with compassion, understanding and a clear direction on what needs to happen here.

A Little Anger Management for Everyone

When anger gets activated within us, we can view it as a blessing, and an opportunity for the body to release this energy that was lying dormant until a trigger activated the emotion needing to be cleared. This is also an opportunity to tap into, or dis-cover, the emotion or event underlying the anger that was being suppressed within the body.
It is an opportunity for liberation, freedom, and love. It is an opportunity to discover your truth. We all have had to numb ourselves down, to hide the truth, pain, and whatever lies we have been programmed to suppress, keeping the fire low, not too big, not too powerful, not too loud, not too wild. Just look at your family, your mom's side and your dad's side, and take a look at how much has been held

in, not acknowledged, suppressed, depressed, and/or projected out. Take a look at the family lineage and what the theme has been in your family. YOU know what it is like staying silent or 'making nice', hoping 'it' will go away by itself. It is like seeing something happen which you know is wrong, yet you don't say anything out of fear, dishonoring your feelings inside. You just let it slide by. It is like dying a slow death inside.

We Can't Stay Silent Any More

What I want to show you is how to free yourself and get conscious with your anger, your fire. Your anger is your ticket to freedom and truth. When you get angry it is never about the other person doing something TO you, but rather about doing something FOR you. If you project or blame the other person or situation, this leaves you as the victim. Release the victim from your life. You are claiming your power in these situations, and that takes courage to stand up and stand strong. This is a conscious, empowering way to look at what is happening in your life.

I want to show you how to capture your truth through the release of anger, and use the triggers as opportunities for the purification of your body temple. You will need to become really conscious of your body. Start paying attention to what your body is telling you. Be willing to honor and listen to your body with love and respect.

Your body holds and remembers all that it has ever experienced. It holds within it all the memories of past wounds and trauma. Just like Mother Earth. In her body she holds all the memories of everything that has ever happened. In her consciousness she holds every negative thought, every emotion that we have ever deposited onto her. She has taken it all in. You have the same cellular memory in your body as the earth does. Think about what the earth does when there is a storm, a fire, or a volcano. She cleanses. It is her nature. You are the same. Your body needs to cleanse and purify just like the earth does. Don't take it personally when the people in your life trigger you: they are gifting you with an opportunity to claim your truth and discover your freedom. Remember, peace is an inside job, and sometimes to get to the feeling of peace and truth, you have to get to the anger in order to release the rage inside.

First, you have to be honest with how you deal with anger. What is your normal mode of operation? Are you in avoidance about it, do you distract yourself when you're pissed off, do you blame the other person, project the anger out, giving your power away? Do you sabotage yourself by not finishing your projects? I have found that many women have a really hard time with getting angry. They're afraid to get angry: good girls don't get angry; it is not 'lady like' to get angry; or it is not spiritual to get angry. It's really hard for men also, because they don't know what to do with anger, and they store it in the body, or blame it on someone else, avoiding taking responsibility for their anger.

Knowledge is power, and to know yourself is one of the most intimate, loving, sexy things you can do.

A Little Anger Management for Everybody

The first thing we do is take responsibility for our own anger, knowing that whatever is triggering us, is offering us the opportunity to cleanse and purify. The trigger acts and feels like a bullet. The bullet is inside you when it goes off. You have control, you are in charge of that fire; you the warrior, the God and Goddess. Within you is that pissed off feeling, ready to release and let go. You are not going to shoot back. You have a choice and you are going to choose a different way.

You are claiming your freedom to choose. You have the choice to do something different with the energy, rather than shooting back. Let's say the trigger happens like the "Mad Dad" in my house. I wanted him out, and he said, "You can't make me". That was a severe trigger. Now let's take a look at the feelings this brought up in me. Let's take a look at the feelings that had been suppressed inside me that were

25

now 'up' to be released through this situation.

Acknowledging and Releasing My Feelings

Kornelia: "I feel scared. I feel frustrated. I feel embarrassed. I feel intimidated. I feel rage. I feel small. I feel insecure. I feel resentful. I feel anger. I feel like I want to shoot back. I feel bullied. I feel powerless. I feel helpless. I feel depressed."

In diving in and feeling all of these these old feelings, they are able to be released and let go. Remember, you are peeling your onion of powerlessness, and once the feelings are gone and released, another layer is transmuted.

When you are releasing old suppressed feelings, they move and flow. They do not last, they change fast, and because you know what is happening and how liberating and freeing it is, you courageously release these feelings and let them go.

Anger Management Room

Next, I am going to go to my Anger Management Room (for example: the forest) to let out all rage. Letting it all out would look something like this: I scream; I shout from the inside out; I howl like a bitch in heat; I dance like I am on fire; I burn away the illusion; I use the f-word many times; and I get that anger out of my body, my temple, my home. This is my alchemical tool. I let the fire get big, and let it all out.

Next, I may also make a call to one or two of my closest friends who have my back. "I need a witness. Can you hold the space?" For me, to speak my humanness, holding the space is sacred work. I will talk about it from all angles, until I am finished and not until then, regardless of something else telling me I should be done with it. I am not done with it until I am done. When I'm done, then I let it go.

The Alchemical Room

When I have acknowledged everything, I am off to my Alchemical Room, where, I get close and personal with my journal. This is where I write out what my lesson was about. This is where unconscious becomes conscious about what just took place, showing me what the lesson was. This brings the whole experience up to a higher state. This is also the time when I make new choices and new declarations: "I choose to be free. I choose to stand in my power. I am strong. I am courageous. I choose to help myself move forward with love."

Such a process takes huge, huge courage and huge compassion for yourself and the person who triggers you. It is not easy, but it works. Be aware that your inner warrior must not project the anger back onto the other person when you are so angry. Get the anger out of your body and then ask yourself what were you angry about. Always bring it back to that: the feeling; the emotion. You will find your truth.

Take a look at the feelings I released during the experience that I shared above. What a benefit this is for me, for the planet, for the 'I Am/We Are Peace Project', for the book I am writing, for standing up for Peace. That experience helped me get my feelings of powerlessness out, and claim my power back. Now my anger is available as creative fire, as fuel for these projects: *ENERGY MADE POSITIVE*.

> *Love, love, love your trigger point.*
> *This is the place where true freedom lies.*
> *Underneath the trigger is your freedom.*
> *Release the suppression*
> *and rise like a Phoenix.*

We can use anger as fuel, as a creative release, and as a form of expression to get things done. This is one of the reasons we are going through so many changes, so that we can use that fire as fuel and make the necessary changes. Releasing anger gives us the opportunity to release limitations from previously perceived states of powerlessness.

It is our choice, it is our responsibility, and we have the ability to respond anyway we choose. When we are in our comfort zone, we don't move to our edge, and nothing changes (because we are comfortable with the status quo).

Yet - everything is changing. Our new normal is change. Use this energy of discomfort to move yourself into making positive changes in your life, moving yourself into a more desired state of peace, love, and harmony. Use that energy for fuel to make changes in your life that would otherwise not be possible.

The conclusion to the story of 'Mad Dad' in my house was that he willingly moved out, one week after having moved in. This experience gifted me with the opportunity to experience a bully in my home and to be able to experience taking my power back. That is no different from any person on the planet being bullied by someone bigger than himself. 'Mad Dad' triggered my shadow, and I thank him for this gift. Our shadow sides are things we don't want to see about ourselves. Our core fear mirrors this to us.

The morning after "Mad Dad" moved out, I wrote a song. I sang. I laughed, and I danced my heart out.

"We have to come together to mirror each other and hold space for each other. We are combining our feelings and our intellect to transmute matter into mystical consciousness. Thank you for mirroring my shadow so beautifully. It hurts so good."

~Kornelia Stephanie

"Our society is more obsessed with the physicality of their looks than the physicality of feeling their feelings, which is the flipside, and the secret to self-acceptance, feeling good, and looking good."

~Kornelia Stephanie

Chapter 5

————∞o⌒⌒o∞————

From Anger to Peace

The key to peace is to release the anger from within your physical body and embrace the freedom that is your truth. Allow yourself to feel everything. Feel it to the utmost without covering it up. Release the feeling and let it go.

The Physical Body and 'Anger Management 101'

The key to peace is to release the anger from within your physical body and embrace the freedom that is your truth. Allow yourself to feel everything. Feel it to the utmost without covering it up. Release the feeling and let it go.

When I talk to clients or people about getting in touch with their anger, it amazes me how many people say to me: "I am fine. I don't have any anger". Or, they say that my talk about anger, my book, would help a person whom they know, bypassing themselves completely. They want to fix the other other person, instead of getting in contact with their own anger. Sometimes the anger is so unconscious, it is buried so deep, they don't even know that it is buried within them. We all have anger, and we all could use 'Anger Management 101'. We all have our own truth to discover, and the best way to do that is to uncover the anger.

If you are claiming any illness in your body, it is an opportunity to discover if and where you are suppressing emotion (anger) in your body. It wants to be acknowledged and released.

Bringing Our Conscious Awareness to Our Body

When we get angry or upset, the event, person, or situation that is triggering us is actually acting as a catalyst to release a feeling that is no longer serving us on our path. This awareness requires courage, and it takes the willingness to look and feel what this is about for us, so that we can release the anger and let it go. What pisses us off, what makes us angry, has nothing to do with the other. Rather, it is up to us to not take it personally. They are the catalyst activating our fire. Because of these experiences, we can use our fire responsibly to create change. We accept and know they are serving us to claim our power, not by force, but through conscious awareness.

Acknowledge the Intelligence and Wisdom of Our Body

By bringing our conscious awareness to our body and using our body as a tool for transformation, we are guided back to our own truth. When we take responsibility and cultivate relationship harmony within our body, we gain physical, mental and emotional empowerment, thus experiencing radiant wellbeing. We are blessed with youthfulness and life. We have the open invitation, if we choose to use it, to get intimate with our body, curious in a dialog, and interested in the messages that the body is ready to share with us. Our body is waiting for us to acknowledge its intelligence and wisdom. Our body is always in communication with us, so we can use it as our best friend who has our back. And, we become our body's cheerleader. The body is our spiritual master, signaling us to engage in a most sensational, intimate relationship. It is the home that houses our Spirit.

We have been unconscious and separate from the intelligence that the body holds. Until now, the societal conditioning and programming has been in place to suppress and ignore our issues. This is one reason why there is so much anger and depression. We have engaged in many possible forms of band-aids, in the form of addictions that cover up what our body is trying to communicate to us. The body knows that it is being ignored and it is expressing symptoms to get our attention. The body is doing exactly what it is designed to do: to be of service. When we decide to honor the messages that our body has for us, then self-healing can take place on all levels.

To prevent the body from getting sick (storing emotions) we need to be open and willing to feel all our feelings, and to not suppress or store any of our feelings or emotions in our bodies.

Why Is It So Important, and How Could Suppressions Show Up As Physical Manifestations

Let's say you are a man, you have a high sex drive, and love to express yourself sexually. Yet, you have a wife who is not sexually expressive; she holds back from physical intimacy. Years go by and you are not getting to express yourself sexually the way you desire with your wife. Time and time again, you get angry and don't say anything, suppressing the energy over and over. Then one day, 15 years later, you end up in the hospital and the doctor tells you that you have prostate cancer.

In the book by Karol Truman, *Feelings Buried Alive Never Die*, she talks about probable feelings causing illness. Repressed anger from being restricted can be a cause of prostate cancer. This is why consciousness is so important. Anger about what we are experiencing needs to be released in healthy ways. In this way it is not held in the body. Anger is not something that is to be feared. It is natural for us to get angry. The key is to be responsible with our anger, to let go of what is out of alignment with us, and to claim and speak our truth.

Live your truth, and love your anger free. Be conscious and open to discovering whatever messages your body is trying to communicate with you. Hold the positive intent to decode the message. Your body will continuously mirror to you, by how you feel, your thoughts and your emotions.

Taking Back Our Power

Your body remembers all of the past trauma, wounds, and pain that it has ever experienced. It remembers everything. It is your job to love your body and get conscious about the messages it lovingly communicates to you. Take back your power. Your body, in combination with your heart, mind and emotions, is your dream machine, the tool that will help you make your dreams come true. The most important thing is to feel good, because feeling good is the fastest way to manifest your desires. Suppressing issues and emotions like anger, or depression will keep you from creating a reality that is in alignment with your truth.

I am so 'over' people projecting their anger onto others. This is unattractive, bullying behavior. It pisses me off. I am also 'over' judgments, slinging back and forth, like a bunch of 3-year olds who don't know any differently. Understand that what pisses me off has nothing to do with you. Do not take it personally if you are a catalyst, activating my fire. This is how I can use my fire responsibly to create change. I accept and I know this is serving me to claim my power, not by force, but through conscious awareness.

Today's Children Are Powerful

I am so over the part that says to hide it from the children. The truth is, they are open and vulnerable to all emotions. They are wired for the New Earth. They can be your bridge. They can be your trigger. They can also be your space holder. The children do not have all the suppressed emotions that you have, and they don't yet have that onion with layers of anger, calling to be peeled off, transformed. Never underestimate our children: they are far more advanced than we give them credit for. They can be your space-holders, holding you after you have had your meltdown. This could be the 'Flip Side'.

I am including a link in the reference section of the book (page 237) for a brilliant video called 'Hanna's Story'. It is one little girl's attempt to life coach her parents. She is trying to wake them up - at the risk of wanting to take her own life. You will want to watch the life changing moment when Anthony Robbins coaches a little girl who wants to commit suicide - and transforms her life forever. I can related to 'Hanna's Story', having experienced such trials in my own life many times. Please do yourself a favor and watch the video.

Anger Turned Inward

Anger turned inward and suppressed can turn into resentment, depression, sabotage, quick to temper, lashing out at people, loneliness, isolation, fear, feeling paralyzed, powerlessness, weakness in the body, holding on tight, shallow breathing, and feelings of lack, limitation, and being victimized.

Depression and Being a Witness

The best thing to do for people who are depressed, be it friends, family members, neighbors, or colleagues, is to reach out to them and get them really, really pissed off! When people are depressed, they have given up. They feel paralyzed, are not able to move forward. They feel lost and defeated. If you know someone who is depressed, let's just call her Jane, go to her, offer her space, offer her your hand, and give her the opportunity to be heard and witnessed. Give her the opportunity to get good and pissed off – to bring that energy from depression up into anger. Ask her what it is she is so depressed about, ask her what she is feeling. Let the anger burn that depression away.

Sometimes we need someone to hold our hand until we can hold it for ourselves. Depression is the lowest of feelings, and people who are depressed could use a hand and a space to be heard. I have seen this work time and time again with clients and friends, including myself. When I feel powerless or feel depressed, it's time to get pissed and get that energy moving. By feeling our feelings and giving voice to our feelings, the need to judge anything falls away, and so do the feelings. Everything wants to be loved, and everything wants to be acknowledged.

Allow yourself to feel everything. Feel it to the utmost without covering it up. Release the feeling and let it go.

Use anger positively as a tool. This will give you energy, creative purpose, freedom, liberation, space, connection, unity, strength, abundance, health, harmony and well-being in your body. This is the best anti-aging cream on the market. Why? Because you are moving the energy, and now new light can move into those cells. You are no longer holding on tight, so you feel relaxed and receptive. Be the compassionate witness for yourself - and others. Bring your awareness to the suffering you are experiencing and allow yourself to be present to your pain, anger, and suffering, without shying away. Let your life be opened by this experience, without resistance.

Two-step Process: Releasing Anger

Step One – FEEL, FEEL, FEEL

An event happens and you get triggered. This could happen in the workplace, in your relationships, or in your environment. Remember, the trigger for the anger is never ever about the person, situation or event. How do you feel about being triggered? Bring the energy back to yourself, and then start the dialog with: "I feel...., I feel angry right now....., I feel upset....., I feel....,". Go deep and bring the feelings up to the surface: "I feel like I don't matter. I feel like I am small. I feel like I am worthless. I feel lied to. I feel cheated. I feel betrayed. I feel I can't trust anymore. I feel powerless. I feel like I have tried everything and nothing works. I feel ashamed. I feel not good enough. I feel afraid to communicate. I feel it in my throat. I feel it in the pit of my stomach. I feel it in my heart. I don't feel loved. I don't feel valued. I don't feel appreciated. I don't feel heard. I don't feel honored. I don't feel safe. I feel disrespected."

Those are old feelings that you are releasing now. What is so awesome about this process is that when you are saying the words, 'I feel', it brings up feelings that will change through this release. The feelings are valid, but they are not the truth. None of these feelings are true, but they are very valid.

This is what not to do!
Some unhealthy 1970's-style ways to express your anger:

- Suppressing the energy in the body
- Projecting onto the other person or event
- Acting like nothing is wrong
- Taking drugs, or drinking your worries down
- Unconsciously complaining or playing the victim role [they did this to me, poor me]
- Going postal, hitting, or harming another
- Sitting in front of the TV and numbing down
- Emotional eating or any other addictive behavior
- Shooting back, or taking revenge at the person that triggered you

This is the healthier path!
Some healthy ways to express your anger (fire):

- Going into your anger management room and letting it out
- Accepting responsibility for your thoughts, actions, and feelings
- Taking ownership for your own anger
- Saying: "I accept, I choose to release, I feel mad as hell"
- Saying: "I am choosing to let it all go"
- Screaming out at the top of your lungs, or screaming your head off!

- Feeling everything from the core of your solar plexus in the middle of your stomach
- Howling like a bitch in heat
- Crying, crying, crying: weeping uncontrollably
- Using the F-word as many times as you possibly can, "I'm so f... pissed off, are you kidding me"
- Stomping up and down, or doing a dance
- Asking yourself: "What am I feeling angry about?"
- Asking a friend to witness and hold the space as you do what ever you can to get the fire out

Allow, allow, allow yourself to feel everything fully; allow yourself to grieve. Allow yourself the space to feel the sadness without pushing to make it go away, or thinking you 'should' feel better. Allow every-thing that is up right now without judgment, allow the change; allow yourself to feel the way you do.

Give yourself this love, this space, this self-acceptance. From this space give yourself that unconditional love and approval.

Feel it all fully, let the energy of it move through you. It will pass. Don't push, but let it all flow through you and fall away.

Step Two – RELEASE, RELEASE, RELEASE

A beautiful blessing you can say now that you have released these feelings is:
"I choose love. I choose my empowerment here. I embrace all of me unconditionally. I choose my power. I claim my life. I choose being at peace. And, I choose to forgive."

Next, take action, grounding in a new and empowered way of being for yourself. You are releasing a feeling of powerlessness and claim-ing your truth. Nothing ever goes away until you feel it all. All has to be felt and released.

If through this experience you released powerlessness, congratula-

tions. What a victory for you. What a gift. Now align with your truth, and make the following statements:
"I choose and claim my power here. I feel so very powerful. I am an empowered being."

Compassion and Forgiveness

After you have had the opportunity to let your anger/emotion out, give yourself some space to really understand what the experience was about for you. What was the lesson, and what approach would you like to take now that you have released this energy?
How would you like to proceed now, having released this energy? You are coming at your situation, your relationship, or whatever it was that brought you to this release, from a new empowered place. What is the most empowering action you can take right now?

Have compassion for yourself and the person who pushed your trigger. Although it hurts and is painful, it helps to remember that the person who triggers you is gifting you. Thanking this 'gifter' for triggering you and mirroring you (your shadow), is a wonderful acknowledgement. Often that takes a while. Offering radical forgiveness to yourself and the person that you feel hurt by anchors your freedom. Thank this person for helping YOU.

The key is to know this, and to apply this awareness after you have taken the opportunity to get your anger out.

Peace Begins Within

'Peace begins within' means taking radical responsibility for being the 'peace bringer' yourself. Learning to release your fire (your anger) is one of the most loving peaceful acts that you can bring to this planet. War is the extreme action of angry people. Even though we have war going on in the Middle-East, and elsewhere, the best thing you can do is to bring yourself into harmony, into a peaceful space within yourself. Be the peace you wish to see. Be a role model for others.

Holding Space for Yourself and Each Other

Holding Space without judgment for yourself or each other is the most loving thing you can do. It offers the opportunity for safety, feeling safe to express yourself without monitoring what is coming to the surface. It is crucial for the person holding the space to not cast judgment. We can hold space for ourselves, but sometimes on the bigger issues it serves us really well to have someone else hold it – being a witness for you and listening to you. One of the greatest gifts we can give each other is holding space and listening. Wholly being present for you, the person who is witnessing you in your pain is also benefiting from the experience. The person whom you are choosing must have the ability to listen deeply without trying to fix or make things better for you. You need to be acknowledged. Everything wants to be acknowledged and met with love and consciousness.

What if the person who triggers you is your partner, your friend, your work colleague, or a family member?

If both of you are conscious of the fact that one person is playing the role of the trigger'er and one is the receiver, the person on the receiving end is being presented with an opportunity to release an old core wound, hurt feelings, or anger. Remember, the releasing of anger gives you the opportunity to release a limitation from a previously conditioned belief. When your feelings are hurt, this is also an opportunity to release old feelings of being hurt, acknowledging this to yourself and to your partner. This is also an opportunity for compassion and vulnerability on your part, and on the part of the person who triggered you. Most of the time the person who triggers you is clueless as to what just took place, and if you bring that awareness and consciousness to your experience, it can be a wonderful opportunity for love, truth and compassion.

Both parties have to be willing, and for the person who is doing the releasing, it is important that you do not blame the trigger'er. This person was your catalyst in bringing up the old wound to the surface for you. This opens up the space for conversation, allowing you to say that your feelings are hurt. Through this experience, there is an opportunity for release.

It's important that the person who triggered you does not feel responsible for your hurt feelings. The best thing this person could say would be: "I am sorry that you were triggered. Can I hold space for you right now? What do you need?" The communication in our relationships becomes more empowered. Everything can be worked through or talked about.

I can promise you that once you release the old energy, you will see the person who triggered you as your greatest gift. When we get triggered by someone we love, we may want to punish them away by withholding our love from them. We want to hurt them back. This is the work of the wounded ego. Withholding your love is hurting you and the other, whereas by releasing the old fear, and then choosing to offer love, you will have transcended the wounded ego.
Thank you so much for being the Peace Bringer.

Faith is a living, bold trust in God's Grace, being so certain of God's promise that you would risk death 1000 times trusting in it.

I have personally experienced this many times in my life, but the last time was when I was all alone, and was about to commit suicide. I was so lost. I had no other choice than to surrender my life. I was a drug addict, had no friends I could trust, was abandoned by my parents. I had burned every bridge I had been walking on. I had nobody. I was so sick that my body had developed hives — burning from the inside out. I was wounded and broken, I had nothing left to live for, and nothing to lose. I had lost all trust in life, and in God.

Love Made Visible

Love just is, without expectation or condition.
Love made visible, not given or taken,
just is simple self-acceptance,
discovered
and allowed.

Love made visible includes all of me,
all my fire, all my pain, all my love,
and all of YOU.

Let there be peace on earth
and let it begin with me.

~Kornelia Stephanie

Chapter 6

The Addict

The root cause for addiction is a lack of love for self and feeling separate from our Source

I was on heavy drugs for 13 years of my life. The core wounds were so deep, with self-hatred at the center. My drugs of choice: crack cocaine and crank. The drugs kept me from feeling my childhood pain, my wounds: the pain and karma with which I came into this life. The drugs kept the lid on and kept me from feeling my worthlessness. My family did the best possible thing by not rescuing me, so that I could hit rock bottom. It was up to me to rescue myself. Choosing to surrender, saying yes to life, saying yes to me, was the hardest for them and me. That was the beginning of my journey and the uncovering of my genius. When I made the decision to ask for help and chose to heal, all the support I needed was there for me. I have always had a very addictive personality and that addictive behavior previously controlled my choices and my decisions. My addictions changed over the years, but underneath everything was a malnourished little girl, starving for love and nurturing. I was addicted to smoking, food, drugs, men, and drama. One of the reasons I chose the drugs I did was because they kept me from feeling. Also, I did not want to gain weight. By staying skinny, I would be accepted. Men would find me attractive, giving me the feeling I was in control. My self-esteem was so low that taking drugs gave me that acceptable, invincible feeling.

I was an 'in the closet' drug addict. I was able to go to work in the early days and keep everything in check. Until I couldn't any more. Slowly, but surely, the self-destructive path took over; I burned down every bridge there was. Both of my parents were alcoholics - the perfect people for me to choose as my parents - so that I could heal my deep core wounds... or not. For me, it came down to releasing my resistance and making the choice to live. Many times I tried to kill myself: by intentionally wanting to overdose, by driving drunk, by staying up for days before a gallbladder operation, hoping I would die on the table. After the surgery I wouldn't wake up. My family had to come into the hospital to talk me back to life.

The pain of facing myself was too much to bear. I believe and know through my own experience that *the core wound and the root of all addictions is a lack of love for self, and feeling separated from our Source.* The form of addiction can be alcohol abuse, drug abuse, emotional eating, codependency, gambling, shopping, and sex. Some people are addicted to drama. I'll bet there are a lot of undercover addictions going on out there in the business world, and in the world in general, causing so much suffering for so many people. Some drugs are legal, and some are not. Some people are addicted to prescription medications that act like bandaids, covering up that which is underneath, just waiting for acknowledgment, waiting for healing, waiting for love. No addiction is greater than the other. *All addictions are the same, keeping us separate from ourselves.* No lie is greater than the other. All lies are the same. A lie is a lie, an addiction is an addiction.

We all have addictive and obsessive tendencies. They are fundamental to being human. Are you chronically dependent on drugs, gambling, sugar, or chaotic relationships? All addicts use addiction as a form of distraction to fill a void, a wound that keeps them distracted from feeling and healing, from getting intimate with themselves.

The pain at the core is feeling separate from Source (from God). It is a lack of love for ourselves. The awakening that is occurring, the light that is coming onto the planet, is triggering people to change, to wake up, to feel, to love everything. People have to be willing to change and to let go and surrender. AND - they themselves have to want to change. Surrendering frees us from our restrictions. It is the only way. Resistance is futile.

Surrendering is Different Than Giving Up

Twenty one years ago was the first time I learned about 'surrender', a kind of surrender that we don't do everyday. I was begging and pleading with God to come into my physical body: "Let me feel YOU. Let me feel YOU Source, because without YOU, I am not sticking around."

I was surrendering my life. This was going to be my final suicide attempt after many conscious and unconscious attempts to kill myself.

I have since learned how to surrender many times. I have experienced many deaths. Surrendering is one of my regular practices. Surrendering into the present moment is the only way to allow something within myself to die and to fall away. Nowadays, I surrender an old belief, an old attitude, or something in my life that has served its purpose. Quickly I give over and release something that is limiting me or restricting me in some way. Each time, this allows me to be reborn stronger, more connected to my own Divine Essence. Death and rebirth is a natural cycle, yet the only way out is going through.

Welcoming the Divine

That afternoon on September 17 of 1993, I was in my living room on the floor in complete meltdown mode. I think God knew I was serious this time, or I knew I was serious. I pleaded with God to take me. I surrendered my life. I had gotten to the point that I could take no more. In my meltdown, that afternoon, of four hours of weeping and crying, I was begging God: "Let me feel YOU. Let me feel Your Presence. Let me know that there is a purpose to this madness in my life."

I could trust no one, nor could I find God in the churches. The real truth: I wanted THE truth. I wanted THE experience. I wanted to fully feel the Presence of God in my body and in my life. I told God: "I have to feel YOU. I promise that I will apply the faith I need to keep going if I have YOU, God in my life."

After a long weeping and pouring out that afternoon, everything changed. I felt the energy, I felt the *Presence*, I felt the Holy Spirit flow through me. Some people have an out-of-body experience, I had an IN-body experience with the DIVINE. After two days of deep sleep, I woke up *knowing* that God was within me, and that now I would be able to handle anything that was coming my way. Somehow I knew that I would be experiencing a deep cleansing, and many things would have to fall away and be taken from me. I knew that I was balancing my karma, and what I was perceiving as loss was a cleansing of my past. There was so much karma to clear from my misguided actions.

My body felt like a kettle that was boiling over, filled with pain, grief, sorrow, suppression, depression, addiction, sexual abuse, loneliness, self-hatred, rage, and so much more for me to feel. Now the job was to empty the kettle and let go of everything – then sit and be empty.

Shortly thereafter, I became homeless. I lost everything: my apartment, my furniture, everything was gone. I was living in a hotel during the beginning of the Christmas Season, when God sent one of his Angels (a maid at the hotel) to offer me a room in her home. For the next year, I lived with two lovely women who accepted a complete stranger into their home, nurtured me with love and food, and allowed me to come back to life.

That was the beginning of a very intense journey of self-discovery, emptying my kettle, letting it all out, layer after layer. I stayed empty for a long while to discover: who am I; who is God; what is death; what do I believe in; where am I going? These were the questions coming from within me that I wrote into my journal.

One day I saw a keychain that said, 'GOD IS LOVE'. I am buying that. This is a belief that I am buying into. God is love, and if I do everything out of love, then that must mean I am serving God - and that is good.

Religion or traditional ways to find God were not my choice. I have always taken the self-discovery, non-traditional route. After feeling God come into my body, I wanted to find out for myself what the truth was. The energy of The Holy Spirit can only be described as 'Divine Grace'. Once you know the truth, you cannot not know it.

My Mission and Purpose

Then, one day three months later, during a cold December winter month of 1993, I was sitting in my room with a blank journal and wrote the following message - as a stream of consciousness:

December 1993.
Guilty myself, before I "surrendered" and begged for a miracle to happen. No faith in life.

I used to live my life, like most people do now, as if there were no principles or truths to follow. Doubts, frustration and despair saturate their minds and they turn to kinky substitutions in a vain attempt to find meaning in life. Drugs and sex are much of the frantic activity they pursue to keep one step ahead of emptiness and loneliness.

What the world needs desperately: we don't need logical arguments to convince us to live our lives to be happy in everything we do. I BELIEVE it's possible. Miracle workers needed to demonstrate and be living examples, in vivid color: flesh and blood people of all races who live in harmony and radiate happiness in all aspects of their lives.

I wish to make the world a better place. That is my purpose and reason for living this life. Source Energy, God's will sent the Holy Spirit to control my daily life. In my surrender, the Cosmic Christ within awakened me, saved me. I am a new leader for our children of all nations in this world, and my wish is to team up with other gifted individuals who are inspired by the Spirit to join me as a team of miracle workers and save the earth.

I have the answer, the greatest weapon of all, and I also have the guts and desire to take on the biggest job that everyone believes is too big for anyone. Of course, that is exactly what inspires me and drives me crazy to prove that miracles happen. It has been said that the cure for all the ills and wrongs, the cares the sorrow and the crimes of humanity, lie in one word: Love. It is the divine vitality that produces and restores life. To each and every one of us it gives the power of working miracles, if we will.

That was 21 years ago, when a wounded woman surrendered her life and asked to feel God, to feel everything, and was ready for the truth. She had to ask, and she had to want it.

I know that my deep desire, and the absolute will to surrender my life, was the catalyst for bringing in the collective 'feeling paradigm', one heart at a time. If you look at this 'mission statement', it might seem pretty corny. However, I see miracle workers all over the planet today creating a New Earth. I also know that many other wayshowers have had these types of experiences. We have had to feel our way into knowing that God as Source Energy is not separate or outside of us.

We are infinitely connected to our Source.

"Something amazing happens when we surrender and just love. We melt into another world, a realm of power already within us. The world changes when we change. The world softens when we soften. The world loves us when we choose to love the world."

~Marianne Williamson

"Surrender is perfectly compatible with taking action. But in the surrendered state, a totally different energy flows into your doing. Surrender reconnects you with the Source Energy of Being, and if your doing is infused with Being, it becomes a joyful celebration of life energy that takes you more deeply into the Now."

~Eckhardt Tolle

"Just for today, surrender yet again – you have nothing to lose but control. How much freer you will be when you let love, let God, have its way with you."

~Kornelia Stephanie

Chapter 7

———∞०८∾○∾০∞———

Victims to Our Bodies

All our life we have been 'victims to our bodies' - until now. We are capable of self-healing and the self-regeneration of our physical body.

Releasing old feelings is the first step to self-healing, and is one of the most empowering, self-loving, nurturing actions we can take to relieve the body of dis-ease.

What we put into our body and how long we hold onto it is our job and our responsibility. All of us have the ability to heal ourselves. If we choose, we can become our own healers and shamans. I embraced this practice and healed my body. When we bring conscious awareness to the root cause of a perceived illness, when we consult our own authority - our own intelligence - we immediately become empowered. The next step is to do everything we can to adopt a wellness approach which will empower us to give our body the nurturing, loving attention it wants from us. Our body is in continuous communication with us, letting us know when something is off. There are many wonderful healing modalities out there, ways that are non-toxic and without all the side effects, all here to support us in the most organic way to claim our healing. Because we have been conditioned to not feel our feelings and to suppress the energy in the body, we go to a doctor when we get sick. The doctor is the perceived authority who gives us a diagnosis, writes us a prescription, and off we go. Did we really get to the root cause of what the body was wanting to communicate with us, or did we just put a band-aid on top? This has been a perfect money maker for the pharmaceutical companies, while keeping people from accessing their true power.

A few years ago, I had my first physical experience of claiming my own authority over my body. I was suffering from two huge cysts on my ovaries. It was very painful and very uncomfortable. These cysts became inflamed on and off over the years. Then it got to the point where I could not take the pain anymore. I had a pap smear and ultrasound done, and I was told the cysts, on both sides, were the size of large lemons. It was very painful and scary. After returning home from my doctor's appointment, I decided that I wanted to heal the cysts myself and that I would do whatever I needed to do to bring about the healing. The first step was to look up what the emotional suppression was: the energy that I stored inside the body, the uterus, or womb over the years. There are two books that I use in my practice which I highly recommend to all my clients: *You Can Heal Your Life*, by Louise Hay, and *Feelings Buried Alive Never Die*, by Karol Truman. Both of these amazing authors address in their books the emotional suppressions and probable illnesses that can cause diseases. In addition, if you want to get to the DNA level of healing, Karol Truman has an amazing Script that she has graciously gifted me to put inside my book for you – located in the back of the book on page 229.

These books belong in every household and every medical office. Wouldn't it be nice if our medical system adopted *emotional therapy* (this natural remedy) as part of the prescription to wellness? This would be fastest way to empower people back health, bringing more awareness to emotional suppressions' harmful manifestations in the physical body. But, until our medical system moves into this consciousness, YOU can empower yourself by reading up on this information.

OK, back to my deciding to heal my cysts.

Step One: Look Up 'Emotional Suppression of Cysts'

Probable cause for the emotional suppression of underlying cysts, a false growth: feeling sorry for self, inability to resolve hurt feelings, running the old painful movie, nursing hurts.

In addition to the above, I came up with my own diagnosis and conscious awareness. A cyst is: a false growth, a boil, anger stored on the womb of creation, suppression in the body, a growth on the inside (instead of suppression expressed on the outside of the body). *The anger was all about the rejection of my own creativity, the suppression of my own creative ideas.*

> Uterus: The uterus (from Latin "uterus", plural uteri) or womb is a major female hormone-responsive, reproductive sex organ of most mammals, including humans.

Taking my power back, I released these stored feelings. I surrendered and let go of the old movie; the old hurt that was playing; and embraced my creative power, knowing I could express my creativity by embracing my creative ideas and not suppressing them inside of the body. Even as I write this story I can see how important this was for me in my creative process, and how this action not only supported my physical body, but also the co-creation of the New Earth. I had to claim my full creative authority, my full creative healing and power.

Step Two: I Canceled My Appointment with Cancer

The next step I took was to phone the doctor's office. Their recommendation was to make an appointment with the cancer specialist to get a biopsy to rule out endometriosis, a female health disorder that occurs when cells from the lining of the womb (uterus) grow in other areas of the body. This can lead to pain, irregular bleeding, and problems getting pregnant (infertility). Because of the relationship I have with my body, I asked its intelligence: "Do I have cancer?" The answer I got back was: "no". I trusted my intuition. Feeling confident with my inner practice, and with my knowing, I phoned and *canceled my appointment with cancer.* I had no intention of buying into the probable suggestive fear.

(I am not in any way suggesting everyone do this. I appreciate our doctors and nurses. By all means, if you need to, seek out a health care professional. Please take care of YOU. That is the most important.)

Step Three: Change My Diet

This was pretty clear. I looked up what I needed to do to change my diet. The first thing that was going to bring me huge relief was to cut back on the carbs and to alkalize my body. Cancer or boils can not survive in an alkaline environment. I started juicing and drinking two green smoothies per day. I also got hold of two energy workers – one was a remote healer, and another was light/color therapist. Both really helped me feel like I was taking charge of my own healing. After releasing the emotional suppression, changing my diet, and working with the natural modalities of my energy workers, my body was free of the cysts. This was a very empowering experience for me.

When we decide that we want to heal and let go, amazing miracles can take place. I remember when my mom, who had a very painful life, developed epilepsy. Her seizures were monitored and kept under control with medication. For a long time that worked, until her seizures became too severe. There were times when she would have about eleven seizures in her sleep. The authorities were even talking about taking her driver's license away, as she was not safe to be on the road. She was too young – not even 50 years old. My step dad and mom went to the doctor and received a life-sentence: she would have to be on medication for the rest of her life, and she would always have epilepsy.

The medication she was taking was Dilantin (phenytoin), an anti-epileptic drug, also called an anticonvulsant. It works by slowing down impulses in the brain that cause seizures. The side effects of being on this drug are pretty severe, from depression to suicidal thoughts, and so much more. This really scared my Mom. One day while my stepdad was at work, she "decided" that she did not want this. She decided she did not want to be on medication for the rest of her life, and that she wanted to live. I am amazed by that story, as my Mom did not have the books to look up the emotional suppression, or know what to do. But, she achieved the same result. She decided she wanted to live, she released the victim, and she chose health. She had to be open for the miracle to happen. She called and claimed it.

These kinds of miracles happen every day, and we are seeing more and more people claiming and having spontaneous healings.

When I look up the emotional suppression for epilepsy, the probable feelings are: feeling a need to persecute self; wanting to reject life; violence against self.

Her strong will to want to live changed her life. She never had another seizure again, and is living a very healthy, happy life. She emotionally embraced her life and was healed.

Anger Suppressed In The Body Is Very Toxic

Let's take a look at the emotional suppression of anger in the body, and just a few common illnesses and dis-eases from the books of Karol Truman and Louise Hay:

- Alcoholism: feelings of worthlessness / self-rejection
- Allergies: feelings aggravated by someone or something
- Arthritis: repressed anger that eats you up
- Colon: bottled-up hate
- Depression: anger turned inward
- Female organs: repressed anger (usually at male authority figures), unresolved resentments
- Liver: feeling of unresolved anger
- Prostate cancer: repressed anger at being restricted
- Pink eye: feelings of anger at present situation
- Plantar wart: deep seated anger

I have a client who when she called me sounded like she had a cold. I was able to tune into her voice, 'hearing' that when she was in the middle of a clearing. I asked her if she had a cold. She said no, that she was dealing with some sort of allergies. By the time we had gotten to the root of the cause, and finished the call, the energy was cleared out of her body. Most of the time she was experiencing a reaction to someone in her life, and called it an allergy. Be very careful of the labels you use for yourself, because your words have so much power.

These are just a few examples to show you illnesses which can be created by storing negative feelings in the body. This is something that happens over time, and therefore it is essential that you feel all of your feelings fully and release and let go of all that which is no longer your truth. Do you see why it is so important to release your anger, and let go? Letting go of your anger can be your cure. When you are working with your body (your best friend) and using your body as a releasing tool, you can feel and experience more pleasure, more peace, and wellbeing. This is a very empowering, loving relationship with yourself.

Gallbladder: Feelings of Anger

I had a client who had severe gallbladder attacks, and the doctors were telling her it needed to be taken out. I encouraged her to release the emotional suppression in the gallbladder. Her family history was one of obesity, and she had lots of emotional suppression in the body. Bitterness and anger stored in any organ can cause disease in the body, and the anger was the destructive force that was not in harmony within. This is always the first place I look.

As her guide and mentor, I encouraged her to embrace the self-healing template and to work on the emotional suppression behind the attacks. We did that together by my facilitating space for her self-healing to take place. If she found she that she did not get the release she needed, then she could still make the choice to have the gallbladder removed.

She successfully healed and released the energy Through that experience she saved her gallbladder and healed herself. WOW! What confidence it created for her in her future. She gained trust in herself, and through that, claimed her power. There are many stories like this.

What do you feel angry about?

"Physical pain is just an extension of emotion.

It's all the same thing.

There are two emotions.

One feels good and one feels bad.

Which means, you're connected to your

Energy Stream

or

you're not allowing

your Energy Stream."

~Abraham-Esther and Jerry

Chapter 8

∽∘৫∾ꞈ∾৩∘∾

Emotional Healing and Self-Regeneration

Time to claim our power, moving into wholeness

We are being presented with extraordinary opportunities to claim our power in every area of our lives. We are releasing the consciousness and core wounds of being victims in our lives – in our bodies and in our relationships. We are releasing the energy of a system of slaves, living in survival mode, controlled by the time matrix. The world, at its core, no longer supports who we are as sovereign beings of love. We are releasing the energy of shame, feeling not worthy to claim our own power. We the people are embracing the consciousness of equality and oneness.

Many women feel fear in claiming and owning their power. As children, many women were conditioned to stay small and not shine too brightly. Now, they are turning their lighthouses on for all to see.

In the old paradigm we were conditioned to not show our feelings: to suck it up and get on with it. Our conditioning was such that if we showed our feelings - living from the heart - we could expect pain. So, we learned to adopt a persona that wasn't authentic and didn't reveal the truth of who we really were. This kept us isolated, separated from ourselves and each other.

Today our men are learning that it is a huge relief, even beautiful, to feel and release their feelings, allowing that energy to move through.

59

They have feelings too. By listening in and allowing their hearts to lead them, they move into wholeness. The men are realizing that getting in touch with their feminine side, their feeling nature, becomes natural to them. They don't need to hide that part of themselves any longer. They are free to openly feel.

We each have male and female aspects and, as we unite the polarities within ourselves, we live openly from the heart, authentically and vulnerably. This unification is a state of wholeness which enhances our being-ness on all levels. The left side of the body is the feminine side (receiving) and right side of the body is the masculine side (actualizing). By getting in touch with our male and female aspects we can observe with increased understanding the qualities that each represent and integrate the polarities within. This alchemical process helps bring us into inner harmony.

In our new world the emphasis is about equality and wholeness, living with a unified balanced heart and mind.

We are meant to thrive and to experience abundance and prosperity in all areas of our lives. All we have to do is say yes. When we find ourselves in situations where everything is, or feels like it's falling apart, we embrace the change and let go of the feelings. This is our opportunity for growth. This is the time for empowerment. No more playing it safe and comfortable. We are not victims. We are empowered creators, and in order for us to know our true power as a creator we have needed to experience the opposite, where we felt limited.

Healing Core Wounds By Using Our Emotions

Healing core wounds by *using our emotions as a clearing tool* is a simple, powerful technique.

Every time you are experiencing a negative emotion you have the opportunity to claim another part of yourself into wholeness and joy. This process will empower you to be response-able for your own feelings and take you out of the victim role. If you are pointing your finger at anyone else, you are giving your power over to them or to the situation that angers you. Take ownership now and claim your power. Own your feelings. All of them.

This was such a huge piece for me. I remember when I first began to take responsibility for healing my core wounds. The healing came through experiencing myself in relationship with the others who had triggered the wounds for me. Even though these experiences were very painful, that was part of my healing. I never thought I would say, "Thank you for abandoning me; thank you for triggering me; thank you for leaving me feeling betrayed by you; thank you for leaving me feeling not worthy."

To best clear these core wounds, they have to be felt and released out of your emotional body. These wounds can be very painful to feel, but it will pass. Emotion is an energy, and once it is felt and released, it moves through, creating space for more vitality and light to enter. *Feeling it is healing it.* Take comfort in knowing that this is a process. You will release the layers of this wound, once and for all. If you get triggered, it is always an issue from the past that needs to be addressed, felt, and acknowledged. This is part of an old wound that is crying out for you to love it, release it, and let it go. Once you heal the core of these, they are gone. Every event is neutral. This is your natural state.

There are really only a handful of core emotional wounds that are attached to beliefs we have about ourselves. We keep repeating the same patterns and having some of the same experiences over and over again. The goal is to be feeling neutral, being in emotional balance. Get conscious with your releasing and clearing. Dive deep and feel all of it. Everything wants to be loved and felt. I want you to know there is nothing wrong with you, and this, too, shall pass.

The Emotional Core Wounds

These are the emotional core wounds that I released and cleared. You might identify with one or more of these: [In the reference section please find a processing technique to assist you in your empowerment.]

Abandonment

I cleared this wound through experiences with relationships where I had felt abandoned, starting in my childhood, feeling abandoned by my father. I was given the perfect opportunities to see where I was abandoning myself, in order to come home to myself, to feel safe within myself, and to honor and value myself fully. Looking back today, I remember there were two friendships where I felt a loss when they ended. I could not understand why they left me, why our friendships ended. Both of these relationships were with my close girlfriends whom I cared about deeply. They probably had no clue that they had triggered this wound for me. Now I am so grateful for these experiences.

A year later, I was in a relationship with a man, and when our relationship ended, abandonment was not what I was experiencing. This is why I can tell you that when you clear the core wound, it is gone for good. It is like it never happened. You are neutral, back to your divine nature. People can come and go and it does not have that effect on you anymore. You have a healthy non-attachment.

Betrayal

Most betrayal wounds have a financial or sexual tie to them. This wound was triggered for me in a close friendship. (Thank God for our friends.) When this wound was first triggered, I was in so much pain. I had suppressed the emotion in my root chakra and could not sit down for two weeks, as this stuck energy was moving through me. As for the friend, we did not speak for a year - until we became friends again - and our next dynamic played out. Our friendship ended again. I recently received an email from her telling me that she was sorry. She said that her actions that summer must have really hurt me, and that I must have felt betrayed by what she had done. I responded that I appreciated her acknowledging her actions, however, I did not feel betrayed as this was not in my field of resonance. I had no cell memory of betrayal in my body. It had all been released. It was not part of my reality anymore. To realize that I was free of this core wound was such a beautiful gift for me. Again, I observed a healthy, neutral non-reactive experience within myself.

Unworthy/Not Good Enough

This has been a deep lifelong wound that is part of many people's experience: low self-worth. This also was part of my healing: I needed to overcome and realize the immense value of being and feeling worthy. I had to experience and heal the opposite and discover the truth within me. The value and worth of who we are is beyond measure.

My childhood had me well prepared to never acknowledge myself, putting my own needs aside. What a long and painful path to claim my worth and love each and every part of myself into wholeness. Today, it's hard for me to imagine that I ever, ever had a thought that was attached to a belief that was attached to the emotion that I was not good enough, and that I used to make choices that reflected that belief.

We are only releasing the feelings of *not feeling good enough through our life experiences* so that we can make decisions that reflect a healthy self-worth, living our highest potential, living our best life, creating and experiencing our life in abundance, claiming our worth, and being with others who reflect our beauty back to us. Feeling worthy, feeling deserving, and making choices that reflect this power must first come from the inside. 'Unworthy', according to the dictionary, means not deserving of attention, value, or respect.

Become aware of anything that suggests that you are not worthy to receive whatever you desire. You are deserving, you do have value, and you do deserve respect. You have been just releasing the opposite feelings. For example, a six-month old baby, who has never earned any money, has never achieved anything, is deserving of value, respect, and attention. You are the same. You are intrinsically worthy. Just like being in the Presence of an Angel; being in the Presence of God (or Source). All deserving and all of immense value. YOU are the same.

Shame (the ugliest one)

We have been conditioned to feel shameful all our lives. Feeling shame is one of the lowest vibrations we can experience. This level of shame is equivalent to death. We want to hide and cover up, we hang our heads, and we wish we were invisible. Early life experiences, such as sexual abuse, lead us to shame, leave us feeling like we are a disgrace, leave us feeling like we should be ashamed of ourselves, like there is a blanket of tar clinging to us.

Being told as a child by your parent or elder "shame on you" caused your personality to withdraw, becoming introverted and shy. Shame is very destructive to emotional and physiological health; it can cause illness in the body and can cause children to be cruel to each other. As an adult, the core wound of unhealed shame can keep you from feeling loved and free, and from reaching for the life that you deserve. Think about how many times you were told as a child, or an adult, "You should be ashamed of yourself."

How do you feel about your sexuality? Another important part of your healing is to release the sexual suppression you have had around our body, the possible shame around sexual abuse, and the limited way in which you allowed yourself to receive pleasure and express your sexuality. *It is our birthright to experience and receive the immense pleasure our body is capable of if we are willing to release and surrender the restrictions.* There are so many wonderful sexuality coaches and educational options out there to assist you in healing your sexuality. It is connected to your personal power.

Please make it part of your healing path. You will be so glad you did.

A few years ago on my radio show called "Empowering YOU," I had a guest who is a sexuality coach. She gave us a practice which invited us to sit naked in front of a mirror as part of a healing around our feelings of being naked. Although it initially brought up a lot of shame, it was a very liberating and healthy exercise. *How do you feel about your sexuality?*

Survival Needs

Most people are in jobs they do not love, living paycheck to paycheck, working robotically to support a lifestyle which may not be in alignment for them anymore. There is always the underlying fear that we can't make ends meet doing what we love. When we move beyond the illusion of our fears, we discover how capable and powerful we really are, how the universe (our co-partner) has always provided for us. We have always been taken care of.

Again, I pushed this survival piece to the edge many times and cleared the lack consciousness out of my being. Lack is not a perception and a chosen reality for me. Freedom is. My core value is freedom: freedom of expression; freedom to live my life doing what I love; freedom that comes with being a creator, choosing my abundance, my flow, and my perceptions. I am in command of my life, and mere survival does not match my integrity. I value simplicity, living my life to my own rhythm, dancing to the beat of my own drum. This to me means I am thriving! Abundance comes in many forms. Abundance is my nature.

Victim/Savior

I have found that being a victim has been the root of my anger: anger because I felt powerless to take full responsibility for embracing the truth of my being as a divine, empowered creator. In writing this book and leading my peace campaign, I faced some of my biggest fears: fear of losing my life; fear of my own rage; fear of failing to make it through. I found myself in many different situations where I chose to release the victim in myself time and time again. One day I faced my biggest adversary and released the victim once and for all. Imagine a woman raising money for peace and standing up for change, in a time when there is so much chaos in the world. This was the perfect opportunity for me to integrate my own shadow, and release the victim for good. I found that I had the courage to approach my counterparts with love, instead of force, with fierce compassion and understanding of the fear within me and them. In the end, I did not lie down and let them walk over me. I released my powerlessness and rose victorious. I am grateful to all who played their roles in perfect support: the light and the dark.

Most people are waiting to be saved by someone. They, too, have a lot of anger, and consequently welcome the beauty of learning how to release the anger, release the victim, and claim their power from the I AM of their being.

Playing the victim and the savior roles are both 'old world'. We don't need to be saved, we don't need to give our power away to someone, and we don't need to force our power over anyone. All we need to do is release the old, claim our Source, claim our truth, and be the love that we all are.

Separation from God/Source

The basis of all fear is rooted in separation from Source. I feel this is what most people really feel angry about: angry at feeling separate and/or abandoned from God/ Source.

If you really want to awaken the God within, release this anger (this pain) out of your body. Your body holds the separation; it holds the trauma, the fear, the pain, and the feelings of separation. This core wound, the mother of all core wounds, is the root cause of the deep sadness, the loneliness of feeling separate from Source (God). Surrender yourself to something greater than yourself. Invite Source to come in and watch the miracle take place.

Separation with Source is just one thought away.

Divine Neutrality

Divine Neutrality is experienced when you have cleared the emotional density out of the physical body, and are no longer in a reactive mode. You have taken full responsibility, feeling completely neutral even when all buttons get pushed. You are in a complete state of surrender in the present moment, knowing all that is happening is divine. The victim no longer lives within. You are conscious of being the creator. You are not even thinking about anything other than being an observer, responding from an organic state, your true divine nature. You are not affected negatively by what is happening in your environment. Even if you are walking surrounded by chaos, you are emitting a frequency of Divine Neutrality. Nothing is 'wrong or right'. It all just is. This is the time when victory is truly achieved, as you are walking in your mastery.

My Own Suffering

My own suffering and pain was too much to bear so many times. It's hard to believe that 22 years ago I felt like I had no way out because deep emotion was attached to a belief of self-hatred and unworthiness at my core. My path to wholeness was to feel and release within my physical body the recorded cell memories of all the deep trauma of my past. Life experiences are stored within the soft tissue of the body and in the DNA. All the physical, emotional, traumatic wounds of the past, including the ancestral lineage, needed to be consciously acknowledged, felt and then released.

Step-by-step, I began to take full responsibility for all that was right before me, every turn, *not pointing the finger outside, but looking within myself* at where I was falling short, facing the darkest parts of myself and my shadow.

I have so much compassion for the souls who find it hard to stay in a dark place, and feel they have no way out. I want you to know you do have a way out. There is a way. It does get better.

The gift: to be united and filled with the Spirit of Grace, merging into Oneness and Infinite Beingness. *I came home to myself through my surrender, and my deep devotion to my sacred journey,* for which I had been preparing all my life. This transformation of the soul through self-mastery is the pathway to wholeness.

I have become a master at processing, and have processed the entire universe through my physical body. What I mean by that is: I process, feel, release and let go of any loss, death, whatever I am experiencing in my reality. I claim my Universe by taking responsibility for everything that shows itself to me, claiming the limitlessness of the greatest power, knowing that it is the contrast which has set me free.

When Does the Pain Stop?

After you clear the core wounds, layer by layer, the pain stops. You move into a neutral space within your being. The wounded child, the one who has been crying for your attention all your life, has now been loved and nurtured by you. The wounded ego has learned to let go of control and trust the Higher Self to be lead from the heart. The victim, after many lifetimes of dedicated service, work and slavery, has been retired and now is free. The addict is no longer looking for something to numb or fill a void, as the addict now has chosen to fill itself with radical self-love; nothing else will do.

> The Wounded Child, The Wounded Ego,
> The Victim, The Addict
> are no longer playing parts in your movie.

Clearing Your Emotional Core Wounds

In the back of the book on page 219, under 'The 21-Day Peace Practice', please find 'Kornelia's Emotional Processing Technique' that I use on myself and my clients. Through the clearing of my own emotional core wounds, I birthed and created the 'Wholeness Coaching Course' (Two Coaching Certification Workshops are facilitated yearly. For more information go to www.korneliaStephanie.com).

After clearing your emotional core wounds, you come back to your neutral, natural state of being. When you reach the rainbow, you see that you are the rainbow, and the reflection is the same. You have suffered so much, and now suffering and struggling is a choice. *Release the struggle, release the suffering.*

The way we heal our bodies is through feeling deeply all our feelings and all our emotions. This is what the pure joy of being in a body is all about: feeling deeply, feeling all of life, fully feeling pain, joy, ecstasy, pleasure, bliss, and harmony. Feeling the contrast of what we are desiring is a gift to us, bringing into harmony the desired feelings and experiences. We express ourselves fully, being vulnerable and opening ourselves to intimacy and deep connection.

We are capable of self-healing and self-regeneration. The intelligence of our bodies has the ability to completely regenerate organs, new skeletal systems, and reverse the aging process. This is what we are all capable of achieving. Our bodies respond to our programming, negatively or positively. By speaking loving words to our bodies, thinking positive thoughts, feeling our feelings fully, and nurturing ourselves back into wellness and vitality with every word we speak, our cells respond in kind.

"We who lived in concentration camps can remember the men who walked through the huts comforting others, giving away their last piece of bread.

They offer sufficient proof that everything can be taken from a man but one thing: The last of the human freedoms - to choose one's attitude in any given set of circumstances.

Life is never made unbearable by circumstances, but only by lack of meaning and purpose. Between stimulus and response, there is a space. In that space is our power to choose our response.

In our response lies our growth and our freedom. It is not freedom from conditions, but it is freedom to take a stand toward the conditions. What is to give light must endure burning."

~ Victor Frankl

Chapter 9

∽oᏨᏨᏒᎧ∽

From Prison to Freedom

From prison to freedom-
that is where we are going

Ιt's up to each of us to claim freedom as our birthright. It takes great courage to speak your truth, stand in your convictions with what you know and be a beacon of light for others to see. Writing this book, baring my soul, and sharing my belief system with the world was a very frightening, yet liberating experience. It gifted me the opportunity to release the fear of being judged, fear of being ridiculed, and also the unveiling of past-life fears of being burned at the stake for speaking my truth. All these fears were cleared through these experiences. It is my hope that by sharing some of my stories, you, too, will feel inspired and empowered within yourself to claim your freedom.

When contemplating writing this piece of my book, I felt incredibly free. Acknowledging my truth, sharing it out loud, standing strong for what I believe in, had me wanting to run down the street with a sign that said: 'I AM FREE'. What I truly value is freedom, and for me that is what this experience on earth thus far has been about: to claim back my freedom. There is no tool with greater power than the joy of embodying freedom with my physical body. Knowing that I am the commander of my ship and that I matter – that I exist – brings a huge smile to my face. My evolutionary journey has been painful, expansive, and worthwhile. What a gift! I see why I was chosen to play this role here with my 'don't give up' tenacity. I was and am so courageous, willing to face the greatest fears – and love them free from the inside out. I am bowing to the teacher in me – and in YOU.

From the beginning, my life's work has been my incarnation, the opening script, my dream and the challenges that needed to be overcome for this embodied soul. There is no greater degree than my own experience.

The Holographic Blueprint

The script: to return to love and peace; to return to freedom; to return to unconditional love; to return to self-acceptance; to create Heaven on Earth.

The challenge: to overcome self-hatred, lack consciousness, slavery, addictions, victim consciousness, and separation from Source - with a big label of NOT WORTHY on the back and the front for this girl.

The dream: to release myself from prison, the inner prison being mirrored back to me by the outside world. They told me someone was coming. I waited and waited for a while, like 30 years or so, then realized nobody was coming and that I had to be my own savior. It was up to me, if and when I wanted to be free. It took me 20 years of conscious work, healing my life, empowering myself, and leading myself out of the
addiction en-slavery paradigm: 'off the grid'"and into a new world.

Living the conscious dream, I have completely reprogrammed myself from negative to positive, making the unconscious conscious in every area of my life. All of my limiting beliefs – where I was programmed in my subconscious, from my upbringing, my family, my conditioning, and by society – were rejected one by one. Gifted by life's experiences, I courageously began to open up and willingly look at the beliefs that kept me in bondage.

Each belief that was not in alignment with my being, and did not honor my integrity to live in freedom, was investigated, questioned, and transformed by me. I chose to challenge the status quo and be true to my integrity as an embodied soul, *living beyond belief.* Making choices and taking actions that *honor my true Divine Essence,* moment to moment, took all of my guts, gumption and courage.

Releasing the En-Slavement Paradigm

Six years ago, I left a very successful career behind, to follow my heart and my soul's calling. I am very glad I did. This was part of releasing the en-slavement paradigm, as I was putting in endless hours of work and feeling like a slave to pay for what I thought was the American dream, the merry-go-round that kept me living above my means. Up to my eyeballs in credit debt, I was as far away from freedom as you can imagine. My soul prompted me to begin questioning: "How do I want to spend the rest of my life?" That was the beginning for me to go out on my own and say YES to passion, YES to living a life that is filled with joy, doing what I love. I began downsizing to live a simpler life. I stopped feeding a controlled monetary system that is built upon dependency on debt loads which are not sustainable. I withdrew my consent. My ego was having severe temper tantrums along the way, screaming in my ears, "what about me," while the wise mother in me was having compassion for the scared ego, not wanting to let go. *Trust yourself. Learn to let go.* Yes, it takes practice and large doses of self-love. It is worth it through and through, because it leads you to peace, self-acceptance, love and more love. I am worth it. You are worth it.

Moving Into Unconditional Love

I am now doing what I love. I am a transformational empowerment coach, living my truth and helping many others claim their empowerment and their truth. My alchemical tools are *my body,* feeling, then releasing the negativity and old feelings, and *my mind,* choosing the positive thoughts leading to a higher vibration and freedom. Using my imagination to dream our new world into being, the single most important asset has been to *imagine things that don't exist yet, and then stand in the faith of their unfoldment, as I move from fear to loving myself unconditionally.* To love myself without judgment, and then embody that love and extend that love to others - that is what unconditional love is. Loving and accepting it all. This especially includes the ones who throw stones and who are against freedom, unity, and peace.

The Divine Marriage

My intense desire for love and my deep passion to experience the highest love in relationship has lead me into unity within myself. The longing I used to have for the connection *within* is no longer separate. This connection is now unified in myself.

I have always felt and known that the greatest relationship possible is the one I have with myself. Making this relationship my primary focus has brought me my greatest deliverance of JOY.

Whatever I was craving outside of myself has dissipated as Connection, Intimacy and Oneness have been unified within by celebrating and loving myself unconditionally. All my burdens from the past have been released, loved free and forgiven. My soul has come home, into my body, in full self-acceptance, fully self-expressed, not needing anything outside of myself to make me feel whole. It brings me profound Joy to share this home which I carry within my heart with others with whom I am in relationship.

In early December of 2009, as an expression of love and ritual, I held a Sacred Wedding Ceremony in my home with a few close friends who came to witness and celebrate my Holy Union with myself. I took the sacred vow to marry the Divine in me, and to love, honor and cherish myself for eternity. Just as any marriage takes work, commitment, dedication and love, so does the marriage to yourself.

The one thing I know for sure is that this marriage will not end in divorce. I now offer Divine Marriage Retreats to share my passion and this love with others. See my website (www.korneliaStephanie. com) for scheduled retreats.

For me, the year of 2014 was the most empowering year of all; the most loving, the most accepting and the most freeing, having released all forms of powerlessness underneath my anger. I went from *victim to victor* and from *anger to internal peace*. Intrinsically knowing my worth and my value, bringing this to life in all of my relationships, feels so natural and organic.

Love is the highest form of expression
Love is the religion
Love heals all
Being the Resonance of Love

Releasing the 'Victim'

I want to tell you a funny little story about the victim. I was releasing a big victimization experience out of my physical body. I was feeling really good, empowered, and strong. That afternoon I ran into a close friend and she asked how was I doing? Guess who answered the question? Yes, you guessed it, 'the victim' answered: "I am so exhausted, I am so tired, I am so over it." She, the *victim*, wanted sympathy. It was such an interesting experience observing myself, I couldn't believe it. When I got home that evening, I asked the victim: "What was that all about? We were feeling good and strong, so why the pity-party?" Then I had a great laugh and went to bed.

It was an automatic habit. I bet that has happened to all of us many times without our noticing. The good news: once you notice the victim taking over, you are on to it; it has no power over you anymore. That is the same with your fears: once you acknowledge and release your fears they lose their power.

When you claim your power, you also empower yourself by accepting that you are your own savior. You are your own authority and your own leader. You make positive choices and take action from there. You release the prisoner, you release the victim, you release the toxic world.

Releasing Fear

In the back of the book, on page 225, I am including a 'Fear Processing Exercise' for you on how to release all your fears. You have heard this before: **FEAR** is **F**alse **E**vidence **A**ppearing **R**eal. The key is to do the work: process and release your fears. This will lead you out of your own prison. You came here to co-create the New Earth, so now be your greatest Self, and do it fearlessly.

> Our ultimate destiny is to be free from fear
> We are brave souls overcoming fear
> Higher consciousness always defeats fear

I heard the other day that the world is encapsulated with so much love right now, and, inherent to the Law of Resonance, all that is not love is being forced to the surface. So, do not dwell on the fears from the outside world, and do not dwell on your own fears. Fear does not exist In the Resonance of Love.

I was talking with a friend who is a game changer on the planet, and he was telling me about his new film that he wants to release in the spring of 2016. It is about taking people from fear to love. We have a lot of work to do to build our New Earth and inspire people into their truth. Many of us are writing books, making music and producing movies. We are the change-makers, the peace-bringers, and the love-holders. We all have been holding this vision and space for a long time, while we have been working on ourselves, undoing our old programs, and being devoted to the evolution of the planet.

Peace Is An Inside Job,

Peace Begins With YOU

September 21, 2014 was 'International Peace Day', and it happened to coincide with my 'Creative Heart Retreat', here in my home town of La Conner, Washington. We connected with millions of hearts around the globe, with the intention of celebrating Universal Peace in Unity, as One, breathing in "I Am, We Are Peace". In the center of our circle we had a beautiful 16-year old woman representing the youth of the world, representing the Divine Feminine. Behind her was a representation of the Divine Masculine and the Elders of our world. Peace on Earth is happening. Each and every one of us now us has the ability to experience internal peace.

The Global Peace Movement was ushered in during the Period known as the 'Harmonic Convergence'. On August 16–17, 1987, all spiritual light workers were called to raise their consciousness. This was a time when more people were waking up, just like the time we are in now: more and more people are waking up and are raising their consciousness than ever before.

'The Global Family' sent out a call for 20 million people to *collectively, at the same time, envision world peace, with the intention of shifting the collective consciousness on the planet.* Jose Arguelles enlisted the help of 'The Global Family' to promote the event: 'Harmonic Convergence'.

> *"Believers in this esoteric prophecy maintain that the 'Harmonic Convergence' ushered in a five-year period of Earth's 'cleansing', where many of the planet's "false structures of separation" would collapse. According to Jose Argüelles, the event came at the end of these "hell" cycles and the beginning of a new age of universal peace." (Wikipedia)*

It was in 1993, five years after the Harmonic Convergence, when I wanted to end my life through suicide. I believe that this was part of *my* cleansing. *Now,* make no mistake: each and every part has subsequently been felt into wholeness, each and every part has been consciously chosen, and each and every part has been loved free. *I invited Source to come into me and cleanse me*, so that one day I could be here as part of the solution, continuing the work of Peace on this planet as a role model: affecting change within myself, thus changing the world, having embraced this miracle, my life, my contribution.

This planet has been gripped by fear and struggle for a long time. The light that is coming onto the planet now continues to illuminate the outdated structures which are ready to dissolve from the inside out. We have had to accept many things which we are angry about. But, I can tell you, once you find internal peace in yourself, nothing can take that away from you.

Reclaiming Our Power

If you have anger within you, YOU are not at Peace. Releasing your anger is one tool that will take you into your experience of peace. You're the only one who can make that change.

Anger has many possible causes: our personal relationships shifting out of codependency; losing our jobs; mass events like worldwide food and water shortage; chemtrails blocking our sunlight; the Fukushima radiation cover-up; biological weapons; mind control; endless wars for profit; GMO food; religious programming; school programming; depopulation. All these use taxpayers' money. It is our time to reclaim our power from within, coming together as communities: standing up for positive solutions; transforming war into peace; transforming fear into love and courage; claiming liberation and freedom for ourselves, our communities, and our planet.

When anger gets activated in us, we can view it as a blessing and an opportunity to release that energy which was lying dormant within the body. Each of us has suppressed so much anger inside, and that which each of us is releasing is individual, as well as collective. This is an opportunity to discover what lies underneath that anger which is suppressed within. It is an opportunity for liberation, freedom, and love. It is an opportunity to discover our truth.

It all begins with US, shifting OUR thoughts, actions, and feelings into peace and harmony. WE are the solution, and evolution. WE are the Love. YOU are the solution, You are the Love.

Peace IS the Flip Side to Anger
Make Peace with Your Piece

Time is Art

Time keeps on slipping into the Now!
The point of power is always in the present moment:
the conscious, present, Now Moment,
with no consciousness - energy - in the past,
because YOU have released all the past
from your physical body and from your experience,
with no consciousness - energy - in the future, which does not exist.
In the future, you're always looking for something
that you think you will get when you get to there.
When you get to the future, you'll be happy, you will have succeeded,
you will have your relationship, and you will have your abundance.
You keep projecting the energy into the future,
which is an illusion,
and keeps you from experiencing the absolute truth
that can only be experienced in the
present moment.
Bring it all into the Now Moment.
this is the place for Freedom, Joy, Abundance,
Power, Creation and Manifestation.
Bring your conscious awareness into the Now Moment
where you merge with your Humanity - Earth -
and bring your Divinity - Heaven - where you meet yourself.
Now do that every conscious 'Now Moment'
and you are 'Heaven on Earth'.

~Kornelia Stephanie

Chapter 10

───────◦◦◦◦◦◦───────

Heaven on Earth

Now that we are free, we have a lot of work to do. We are building our new Earth, there are many changes taking place, and so much more will change. Every single experience in life gives us the opportunity to clear, and let something old that is no longer our truth, fall away, so we can claim our truth within our physicality and create a more harmonious way of life. Writing this book about peace, and the intention to ask for world peace, first had to be experienced within myself. I truly know that in order for me to want something, I have to be a matching vibration for it.

To have and experience peace on this planet is our birthright; it is the wish of all the children to be able to learn, live, and grow in peace. This planet is our responsibility, to be good Earth stewards, take care of our land, and each other.

Now that we are free, we can create and build our new world. All along, the divine plan has been to birth a new world into being, co-creating with many others who hold the vision and imagination. *You can have anything and everything, even a whole new world to live in.* That time is now!

Heaven and Earth is inside of you, inside your physical body. There you have everything you need. Let go of all struggle, shame, pain, guilt, control, and claim your freedom.

The Keys To The Inner Kingdom

- · Feel all your feelings, (feeling it is healing it)
- · Allow your body to rest
- · Think positive thoughts
- · Spend as much time in Mother Nature as possible

Love, love, love all the trillion cells that are within your body. Open your heart and listen. Let your heart lead, say your daily "I loves" to yourself, offer your presence and acceptance to all that which you feel, and by all means invite that inner child of yours to come out to play.

As conscious co-creators of our reality, the Divine Plan and the Highest Vision is for us to co-create our New World – building a foundation with a brand new consciousness that is rooted in LOVE and PEACE. Do it for yourself and do it for all the children. We are all one.

So How Do We Do It?

It begins with each and every one of us. It begins with YOU. You are all masters. You are not victims. I encourage you to reach into the realms of living your highest potential here on Earth. Bring your unique expression of your true Divine Nature. That is why you came here: to live in freedom to be YOU; to co-create our New World; to build a foundation with a brand new consciousness that is rooted in unconditional Love and Freedom.

Each one of us has our own unique expression that is ready to be realized and grounded in the New Earth. We are limitless. This is the *Truth* and you are the creator of your own reality. Imagine yourself as Source Energy living your highest vision.

Through your daily commitment and devotion to love, beauty and truth, you inspire and develop individual leadership and collective greatness.This develops into personal radical self-love and empowerment. You inspire and empower others through your example to live from your heart. You stand in your power, passionately speaking your truth, expressing your true feelings, communicating with clarity, and using your voice to speak up and create a reality which is rooted in Love.

Our mission is courageous, as we take responsibility for ourselves individually first and foremost. We know this is how we will affect change collectively. We support and encourage each other day by day. We embody peace from within, and we shine on, bringing the highest version of our self to our community. We know that self-love, unconditional love, and self-acceptance are primary. We are limitless beings who journey in freedom, step-by-step toward self-empowerment, inspired leadership, prosperity, and love. We are conscious, creating our new Earth community through the heart connection, through our love for each other and our planet. We know we are greater together than we are apart. We come together in unity and peace.

I AM, WE ARE PEACE UNIFIED

Can you hear your heart calling?
Are you ready to Thrive?
Is Freedom calling YOU?

My religion is *love of the highest order*. My priority is love, to be love in action in all I do, give, and express.

It has been part of my evolutionary journey to be a bridge, to be the rainbow, to shine my light and be a beacon for others; to realize Heaven and Earth within my physical body, to harmonize all disease from within, then balance, stabilize, and anchor-in this Light.

May it be of service to all others who are ready to accept their truth, their freedom, their liberation and accept full responsibility for themselves.

May all beings, all races, all colors, all religions and spiritual traditions come together in Unity, offering each other Peace, Compassion and Love.

I want to thank you so much for reading this book and being the peace you want to see in our world.

I am inviting you to commit to the following '21-Day Practical Peace Journey', designed to support you to become better acquainted with yourself, to help you release old feelings, to inspire and empower you to discover your own personal truth: to enable you to relax into the wonderful being you really are.

Are you willing to make 'Peace of Mind' and
'Peace of Heart' your primary goal?

Part Two

The Peace Practice: Making Peace with Your Piece

"Man is ever searching for his Divine Self and thus in searching he will someday find his Self and God as ONE."

"When we use the term SELF as applied to man, we mean the divine spark of God awareness which serves the physical body from the cosmic Light of Mind. The discovery of one's Self, therefore, means the discovery of one's divinity which unites man with God."

~Walter Russell

The Peace Practice

Introduction - Making Peace with Your Piece

I n the first section of this peace practice, I again cover the power of emotions and repeat the basics of emotional understanding. Please bear with me. We will get to the peace practice. As Human Beings, repetition serves us and strengthens our practice. There is nothing more important than understanding how to be a fully realized Human Being, feeling all emotions fully without repression, suppression or numbing your feelings.

I don't want you to rush through this process, and I encourage you to take your time. I want you to understand your emotions. I want you to absorb this information, as these are the greatest tools you have to enrich your life and to support your emotional well-being. Without this knowledge and the experience of how to use your emotions as a tool to liberate and heal yourself, you will continue to feel victimized. Using your emotions - your life experience - as a guide to liberation, these practices deliver the key to enhancing your well-being, improving your health as you claim your power in all areas of your life.

You have the wonderful capacity to deeply feel all of your emotions. It takes courage and a willingness on your part to allow yourself to feel the discomfort of pain and suffering - whatever it may be. It is easy to feel Joy; it is more difficult to consciously feel loss and feel sadness which is part of being Human.

I promise, you will learn to become an expert in processing your emotions! You can become your own inner doctor, your own nurse, your own coach. You will enjoy applying this process once you see how it works, leaving you feeling happier and more at peace than you ever would have thought you could feel. You deserve to feel all of your emotions. It is part of Being the New Spiritual Human.

An Introduction with Practical Tools
to the 21-Day Peace Practice

Are you willing to make Peace of Mind
and Peace of Heart your primary goal?

This is your special invitation to set out on your own individual '21-Day Practical Peace Journey'. Here you find daily inspirations along with all the practical tools to help you become more intimate with yourself, aiding you in releasing your anger, liberating yourself into your own truth, thus making PEACE with your PIECE.

To assist your '21-Day Peace Practice', take advantage of the user friendly online journal available on my website at
http://www.korneliaStephanie.com/onlinejournal.html.
This journal, downloadable as a PDF, will offer you space to write in and doodle, as you dive in and allow all your inner wisdom to come out onto the page. You can reflect back daily, seeing the progress you have made on your intimate journey to inner peace. Each day you will have more discoveries as you seed your new garden with love, peace, and purpose. You may also use the book to write in.

You will love this process. Enjoy and have fun.

What To Look forward To and What To Expect

The peace vibe is now so contagious that the hearts of millions of people everywhere are experiencing ecstatic symptoms of inner peace.This inner movement is rippling out in staggering proportions, so that for the first time in the recorded history of this planet, we are experiencing Peace on Earth, one heart at a time.

A Few Symptoms of Inner Peace

- Undeniable feelings of freedom in every moment
- Walking the middle path, neither for nor against
- Uninterested in judging yourself or other people
- Uninterested in pushing an agenda
- Uninterested in holding yourself back
- Uninterested in conflict, worry or struggle
- Uninterested in wanting or needing validation from others
- Spontaneous outbreak of laughter and dance
- Overwhelming romantic feelings of love in each moment
- Experiencing so much flow and abundance to share with others
- Consciously allowing things to happen, rather than making things happen
- Laughing so hard you cry
- Feeling connected with nature and others
- Creating and expressing your love with others and all of life

Peace

- One of the highest vibrations possible
- Harmony of spirit, being and feeling totally open and relaxed to receive and experience many states of being in which your body thrives
- Feeling centered, tranquil, inner calm

When you feel at peace, you experience being ageless, timeless, and unlimited. When you are at peace, you experience perfection in freedom, and oneness with all of life. In these next 21 days you are going to change your life and change your habits as you begin a positive lifelong practice that works for you.

Congratulations On Becoming A 'Warrior of Peace'

What does that mean? It means that you will be the one who will choose a higher path. It means that you will take ownership of your full authentic power and truth, lead by your compassionate heart - even when others do not. That is what a true warrior does.

Thank you for making a commitment to take full responsibility for the practice of peace. This will make a huge difference in your life, in your relationships, and your community.

To really know what peace means to you, the following journaling practice will offer some insights into yourself, lightning bolts of awareness, as well as practical tools and practices which will give you the information you need for when you get triggered – which YOU will – and how you will be able to respond in an empowered, conscious way to that which is happening in your reality and in your body.

Practicing peace is taking full ownership for everything, including your anger, not projecting your potent energy onto other people or events (leaving you as the victim and them as the bad guys). We can not fight war with war. We can, we will, and we must offer compassion, understanding, and love - for ourselves, and for each other.

> *"Holding onto anger is like grasping a hot coal*
> *with the intent to throw it at someone else;*
> *you are the one who gets burned."*
> *~Buddha*

In the end, it is always YOUR anger. Underneath that anger are feelings of powerlessness, waiting to be released. Strength is to be gained, along with the rejoicing in your truth and the acknowledgement of your own liberation. There is gold in that.

Being a witness to the shift in your own life, as you are embracing this change to being your greatest self, your body is going to feel so much lighter and feel more at peace as you are strengthening your inner muscle, clearing and pulling some inner weeds as you get started. May you bring your peace, your gratitude, your love, your consciousness, and your joy into each and every present moment.

We are limitless infinite beings creating our own reality each and every moment. It all begins with our physical bodies. It all begins with YOU.

In practicing inner peace, you are breaking old patterns and letting go of limiting beliefs which are no longer in alignment with your essence. You are addressing underlying emotional and physical issues, so you will be able to achieve and live a lifestyle which has you feeling deeply peaceful. You are learning to listen to your body communicate to you when there is stress or dis-ease. Releasing old feelings and choosing peace is the work.

You are responsible for your life, your happiness, your reactions, your actions, your relationships, your environment, your body, your health, your thoughts, your emotions, your feelings, your nutrition, and your well-being. It is your life and it is all up to you. Nobody can do this for you. You have a great opportunity for your own personal empowerment by accepting full responsibility for everything which you are creating in your life.

Being a warrior of peace is your responsibility. I define responsibility as your 'ability to respond' to whatever is happening in your life. How you respond to whatever is happening in your life enables you to see if you are still reacting to old issues, whether you are neutral, or if you are now choosing to respond from a place of empowerment - instead of victimization, blame, and judgement. When you stop judging others (including yourself) and stop blaming and pointing the finger at them, you are being responsible. This puts you in a place of power. You are not a victim. You always have a choice. Taking responsibility and full ownership for everything in your life – all of it (you created it) – enables you to un-create it and create something new. Being responsible for your life and choosing to respond in powerful ways sets you up to be in charge of all of your creations and puts you in the driver's seat. Again, it lets everyone off the hook. You are the master of your energy, taking full responsibility for your actions and experiences.

Where do you feel you need to accept more responsibility?

I Joyfully take full responsibility for my Life

Being warriors of peace demands commitment. True commitment means giving your word to yourself and keeping it. Honoring yourself should always be your highest priority. Your commitments should support unequivocally your evolution and growth. Make a promise to yourself to value any relationship in which you are involved. Put yourself first in all actions, decisions, and agreements. Really wanting to be 'there' requires you to invest your own energy there. And, knowing that your energy is valuable, you only commit to something that you really want to see through to completion, honoring your word. It is your promise to yourself to be loyal to something which is important to you. When making a commitment, you are making a commitment to yourself.

Are you ready to reclaim your level of commitment?

I am a Success with my Clarity and my Commitment
Being a warrior of peace, and practicing peace, requires forgiveness. Making forgiveness a regular practice will keep you feeling light and free. As with the word commitment, forgiveness begins with

ourselves:– forgiving ourselves for all the places we have fallen short in the past, for all the spaces that were left untouched, just waiting for you to forgive in yourself so that you could begin again with a lighter load. While you are there, forgive everyone everyday for everything – especially the ones that you feel hurt you in the past. Being compassionate and offering forgiveness is the path of the peaceful warrior. You are the one who is carrying the heavy load, and letting others off the hook frees you up to get busy creating your life, and experiencing your JOY.

So with that said, let the chant be, "I forgive myself. I forgive myself. I forgive myself. I let it all go." Even if (and especially then) you fall off the wagon on your commitment, forgive yourself and begin again. "I forgive myself. I forgive myself. I forgive myself."

What do you need to forgive yourself for?

I forgive myself for everything, everyday

Being a warrior of peace, you must live and be in integrity with your truth in order to live and be your authentic self, to stand firm in your truth and in your convictions. Letting go of so much old stuff – emotions, beliefs, habits, and patterns – brings you deeper into your truth. What is true for you today may not be your truth tomorrow. This is why it is essential that you are in alignment with your highest principles, values, and integrity, being honest with yourself and others, treating others fairly, and living with honor. When you are not acting with integrity you will feel a nagging inside, telling you something is off and you are out of alignment. When you are in integrity you will be peaceful and have assured clarity of your truth and right action.

Breathe into your heart and take a look at where you may be out of alignment. Which situations create those uncomfortable feelings within that let you know that you are not in peace and harmony with your truth?

I act with clarity and live life with Integrity

Choose To Think Positive Thoughts

You need to learn to select your thoughts the same way you select your clothes. Every thought should be radiant with love; Speaking words vibrant with love. All actions should be cultivated by the power of your thoughts. That's the only thing you should be trying to control, work on your mind.

The Secret To Feelings

Daily, you are being provided with plenty of experiences and opportunities to release old negative suppressed feelings. The secret is to feel the feelings. All of them. Acknowledge and release the negative feelings so that the positive feelings can enter. The secret is to bring your consciousness into whatever you are releasing. Empower yourself. You can't have the negative and the positive in the same space. Remember, by releasing negative feelings of, say, 'failure', you are stepping into the wiser side of yourself which is learning from all that has happened. This is the place of Power! Feeling good is our desired state; it is also the most optimal place for us to experience our joy, vibrant health and our abundance – daily.

But Why Do I Feel So Bad?

Part of loving ourselves is accepting ourselves, even when we do not feel good. Doing some inner housekeeping is part of our self-love journey. We need to get conscious and reach down to the roots and be brutally honest about what is crying out to be loved free. Sometimes we are ready to release and let go of an emotion that is attached to a belief. Let's take a look at our emotions.

What Is An Emotion?

Emotion is energy, or it can be described as 'Energy in Motion'. Emotions are the paintbrush that is painting your canvas of life. Emotions are how we express our energy. We are either expressing happy emotions or negative ones, and it is important to release the negative emotions out of the physical body in order to experience our natural state. When we are suffering, our emotions show us when something is out of alignment with our true nature, and they keep us on track by signaling when we need to check in with our heart. Emotions are our guides! We use the energy of emotions – expressed through our physical bodies – to feel and create our best life.

Expressed Emotions

An emotion is an energy, and once it is felt and expressed, it moves through you and out of your body, creating space for more vitality and light to enter. When an energy/emotion gets expressed, it moves. Energy is fluid. When an energy/emotion gets suppressed, it causes stress in the body. It can cause physical pain and eventually dis-ease.

Think about when you are angry: how do you hold that energy in your body, and where do you hold it? Ask yourself, "Where am I feeling this in my body?" Negative emotions that are felt and released provide natural healing for us. Feeling the pain is healing it.

Two Types of Emotions: Love and Fear

The loving, positive emotions we feel are: joy, happiness, peace, compassion, freedom, allowance, acceptance, willingness, support, confidence, playfulness, worthiness, trust, and abundance.

The fearful, negative feelings to release are: anger, guilt, sadness, rage, resentment, anxiety, depression, doubt, hurt, pissed off, sabotage, abandonment, unworthiness, betrayal and shame.

We express or suppress our emotional energy by choosing love or fear. Each day we make thousands of choices based on love or fear.

Are you choosing loving emotions, or fearful emotions? Take a few minutes to notice how you are feeling right now and put a word to it. If you are feeling a fear-based emotion, ask yourself why you are feeling this way.

Emotions Are Your Tool For Liberation

Using our emotions as a tool for clearing old wounds and releasing negative feelings is a simple yet very powerful technique. Allowing yourself to feel the pain and the emotions, fully without judgment, is taking the first step in the healing process. Every time you experience a negative emotion, you have the opportunity to claim another part of yourself into wholeness and joy. The key here is to acknowledge your feelings. You are the only person who can do anything about how you feel. Are you expecting your partner to acknowledge how you feel?

How Men and Women Have Been Conditioned

When we suppress our emotions, those very emotions are amplified through a continuous feedback cycle. This type of conditioning appears to be true for a lot of men in our society; they have been raised and conditioned to not show their feelings.

Men suppress their emotions and feelings, not connecting to their heart-space, mainly because of the belief system that it is not masculine for a man to cry, or show his feelings. The opposite is true: showing our feelings and processing our emotions makes us strong. We honor ourselves. It makes us human and opens us up to being vulnerable, approachable, allowing love in. Men have also been conditioned to 'suck it up': get on with it; be strong. Men have feelings and need to express them. Maybe not as emotionally as women, but men do like to talk about their feelings. If not, unexpressed emotions can lead to rage, wars, violence, physical illness, and all sorts of destructive behaviors.

Women, who by nature are very emotional beings, have also been conditioned to not show their feelings, to put on a good face, to put food on the table, to take care of the kids while working full time jobs and running household (sometimes all by themselves), often with no space to be heard. They have been conditioned to be strong, not to cry, while not feeling safe to express and share their feelings with each other.

Unexpressed emotions in women and men can cause depression, powerlessness, victimization, anger, rage, and physical illness in the body. A result has been that women and men often deny their own power and strength.

Handful of Core Wounds

There are really only a handful of core emotional wounds which are attached to beliefs we have about ourselves. We keep repeating the same patterns, resulting in the same experiences. As Einstein so famously quoted: "Insanity: doing the same thing over and over again and expecting different results". Until we are ready to wake up and release these old limiting patterns which keep us stuck, we are truly insane. It's critical that we are in emotional balance: either feeling neutral or experiencing bliss.

Core Wounds:
- Abandonment
- Shame
- Betrayal
- Unworthiness/Feeling Not Good Enough
- Basic Needs Not Met
- Victim/Savior
- Separation from God/Source

Core wounds need to be felt in order to be cleared out of the physical body. Feeling into these wounds can be very painful, but that will pass. Emotion is energy, and once it is felt and expressed, it moves through, creating space for more vitality and light to enter. Feeling it is healing it. Take comfort in knowing you can release this wound once and for all. I have found that being a victim has never caused me to feel deep emotional pain; however, being a victim is also a core wound that needs to be addressed.

Every Event Is Neutral

Every event is neutral. This is your natural state. If you get triggered, it is always an issue from the past that arises to be addressed, felt, and acknowledged. This is part of an old wound that is crying out for you to love it, release it, and let it go. How would that show up in your reality?

An event takes place in your life and you get triggered emotionally, finding yourself in the middle of a meltdown. Your first reaction is to lash out or blame the situation or other person However, viewed from a different perspective, what took place is your opportunity to clear emotional baggage from the past. Let's say you applied for your dream job, one that you wanted more than anything. You went all out to get it, and you had your heart set on it. The interview process went well, and they told you that you had made the short list. Then the next day you receive the email informing you that they had chosen someone else. Breaking down in tears, you have an emotional release. You begin to question yourself, your abilities, and come to the conclusion that you are just not good enough and nothing ever works out for you. This feeling of not being good enough, or not qualified enough, triggers in you the core wound of feeling unworthy.

Clearing the Core Wound of Unworthiness

Central to this core wound is a belief that says: "nothing ever works out for me".

Getting to the core wound of unworthiness is like peeling the layers off an onion. Release the feelings, 'I am not good enough' and embrace the new belief, 'Everything always works out for me'. It is as easy as that.

If you are able to stick with the process long enough, you will be able to identify and then clear this core wound, because the truth is: you are deserving and you are worthy. Knowing and understanding that you are clearing this core wound is both healing and empowering. Once you are able to clear this core wound (think onion), you will come to a place of feeling deserving and feeling worthy. This is based on the actions that you continue to take towards receiving all the goodness into your life, knowing you deserve nothing but the best. Feeling worthy and good enough, you embrace success on all levels.

Every person is worthy and deserving. It is up to each and every one of us to realize this. Nobody can do it for us. It does not have to be proven: we are worthy.

True worth comes from knowing inside that you
deserve the best. You expect it.

Your Buttons get pushed

If you are being triggered emotionally by something or someone, you are likely feeling upset, angry, hurt, withdrawn or depressed. This is your first clue to pay attention to how you feel.

Now you have the perfect opportunity to clear this emotion/feeling. Know this: anytime you are emotionally triggered by something, it is always, always something from your past. It is never from the present moment. If there were not a wound somewhere, or an emotional charge, you would not feel that much pain or anger. Think about when you are angry; where do you hold that energy in the body; should you change how you feel? First, there is no 'should'. How you feel is how you feel. This needs to be honored and acknowledged, no matter what.

> *Appreciate your triggers. Appreciate*
> *what and who triggers you.*
> *You are being gifted with a great*
> *opportunity to release old*
> *suppressed, limiting feelings.*

How to Accept Responsibility For Your Emotions

First, choose to respond in a conscious responsible way, clearly feeling your emotion.
Secondly, stop blaming, projecting, and judging others. Stop pointing the finger at them, saying: "you are doing this to me". That holds you in the victim role. When you accept responsibility for your own feelings, you will share all of yourself from a non-judgmental, empowered space. Can you imagine what would happen on earth if we all took responsibility for how we felt? Every single negative emotion has been deposited onto this earth like trash. One of the most empowering things you can do is accept responsibility for how you react. Stop the cycle.

Are you being attentive to yourself?

This process will empower you into being response-able for your own feelings, releasing you from the victim role. Just think about this: *who really is responsible for your feeling anger? If you are pointing the finger at anyone else, you are giving your power away to them, or to the situation that you are angry at.* Take ownership now and claim your power. Own your feelings. All of them.

Beliefs and Emotions Shape Our Reality

Our beliefs and our emotions determine how we shape our reality. We manifest our desires through our emotions and our beliefs. Through conditioning, most of us have learned ways to repress, hide, or set aside our emotions. Emotions trigger thoughts, which trigger more emotions. These thoughts are attached to a belief with which you no longer resonate and that wants to make itself known to you. A simple 'self-inquiry' will break the endless cycle.

What Is Processing?

"Processing is a form of self-inquiry, a way of looking at our egoic self. "Ego" refers to the personality structure, which results from childhood and worldly conditioning. The term "to process" means to examine and to inquire deeply into the nature of our conditioned and unbalanced egoic programming with the intention of moving our awareness into balance and truth. We process our consciousness in order to become clear and ultimately to find our wholeness."
~Leslie Temple-Thurston

The Peace Practice

What is Emotional Processing?

This practice is to be used on a daily basis to clear yourself and to quickly transform issues, providing that you are willing to be conscious and feel your emotions (energy) fully, accepting responsibility for your own feelings. End reacting to that which triggers you and stop projecting your reactions onto someone or something else. This is one of the most empowering things you can do for yourself. Choose to use your emotions as a tool to clear and liberate yourself into wholeness. YOU are your own 'Guru.' Nobody else can do this for you.

Your Emotions, Your Anger, Your Catalyst For Release

When anger is activated within us, we can view it as a blessing, an opportunity to release from the body the energy that was lying dormant prior to the activation or trigger. This is an opportunity to discover what lies suppressed beneath that anger. It is an opportunity for liberation, freedom and love. It is an opportunity to discover your own truth. Each of us suppresses anger inside—'how much' being different for everybody—and what each one of us releases is individual as well as collective.

What To Do With Your Emotions

Being able to identify what people do with their emotions is vital. The question must be asked: "How do I cope with and express my emotions and my energy?"

There are four ways in which a person can express or deal with emotions, and knowing how you, or your client, deals with them shifts the balance of power from the emotion, back to the person.

> *Suppress/Deny:* Trying to hide the emotion from yourself or trying to avoid it
> *Withholding*: Being aware of it, but consciously choosing not to express it
> *Unconscious Expression:* Dumping it on another, or blaming another
> *Conscious Experiencing/Expressing:* Willing to feel the emotion fully with clear expression and self-responsibility

In order to heal a core wound, choices must be made that will counteract a particular wound, and it is from this perspective that one is then able to make choices that reflect the exact opposite—then embody these choices. The ultimate goal is to move beyond duality into wholeness. It is from the place of wholeness that a person is able to stop thinking in terms of black or white, right or wrong, and, through neutrality, to begin living in a space where there is nothing to fix: where the only thing necessary is to heal and become whole. *Releasing feelings is the key: by releasing feelings of abandonment, not feeling good enough, feelings of betrayal or other negative feelings in your relationship, you are stepping into that wiser part of yourself, knowing that you are learning from all that has happened. This is the place of emotional power.*

If we feel:	We want to feel:
Abandonment	Safe
Betrayal	Trust
Unworthy/not good enough	Worthy (You were born worthy)
Survival	Abunndance and flow
Victim/Savior	Empowerment/Creator
Separation from God/Source	Oneness and Unity

Shame (the ugliest one)   Shine

If you do not wish to write in this book, we invite you to use our on-line journal, with the accompanying audio. OR, write your answers in a journal or on a separate piece of paper.

When You Get Emotional, What Do You Do?
What Is Your Coping Strategy?

Do you go shopping, eat or overeat, drink or do drugs, clean the house, busy yourself to avoid looking at what you are feeling? Do you go to the gym and exercise like crazy, or go back to work so you don't have to think (feel) about what's up for you? What do you do to avoid yourself?

Every Negative Feeling Wants To Be Felt and Released

Be willing to go in and feel the pain. Feeling it is healing it. Is it going to be uncomfortable? Yes, it is. You have to be willing to feel the discomfort and the pain. After the emotion has been felt and expressed, it naturally moves through you and creates space for new things to come into your life. If you are willing to take ownership for what you are feeling, you will empower yourself right before your eyes. Your life is about to change from living as a victim to being a powerful co-creator. Are you ready to really understand and experience how powerful you are?

Daily Processing

To help you learn to self-dialog when you get triggered, I have created a daily processing technique that is in the Processing ToolBox at the end of 'The 21-Day Peace Practice'.

Once you begin clearing your emotions on a daily basis, you will notice how much more joyful you are and how simple feeling your feelings really can be. You will begin to notice when you are feeling off, and you might ask yourself: "Why am I feeling off? What is this about for me?" Checking in with yourself will result in your feeling powerful and free. Every situation in life and every experience is there by your own creation. Taking ownership for everything that shows up will set you onto the path of emotional liberation and freedom.

Embracing Your Wholeness

Embracing wholeness is about choosing and embracing the consciousness to love all aspects of yourself, even those that you would rather stuff into that backpack labeled 'ignore,' falsely believing you can bypass 'that one,' thinking: "It won't matter anyhow." In the process of embracing wholeness, you are allowing the parts of yourself that are no longer in alignment with your true self to fall away. Each time you release an old thought or feeling, doing so consciously, you are bringing home another part of yourself, and you are taking another step closer to personal wholeness and freedom. When you embrace your wholeness, you are choosing unconditional love for yourself and others, and in the process, you are allowing more love to flow through you out into the world. Your thoughts and your beliefs create your reality! Unfortunately, we inherit other people's beliefs and sadly make choices that reflect those beliefs on a daily basis. Ask yourself: "Who is running my show? Is it me? Or, is it those messages I have received throughout my life (that I believed) telling myself that I am not good enough, smart enough, worthy enough, or sexy enough?" You can choose to change these beliefs, and in doing so, create a belief system that is more in alignment with the real you.

Core Beliefs

Beliefs are thoughts that we think over and over and over again. Most of our deeply held core beliefs are subconscious impressions, received before the age of seven when we were openly absorbing all the information around us. By exposing our deepest hidden beliefs, we are able to transform them into new empowering paradigms, and create a life that is in alignment with our highest potential.

Negative Core Beliefs

All negative beliefs are lies, and not your conscious choices! Your subconscious has been negatively programmed by your conditioning. You have the power to transform your subconscious programming into a positive belief system. You have the power to change that now!

Negative Core Beliefs About Relationships, Money, Our Body, and Our Jobs

The following beliefs are some that are on automatic pilot in the subconscious. Some were imprinted before the age of seven, and others are the result of experiences relived over and over again. You make choices based on those old imprinted beliefs.

Can You Relate to Any of These?

- Men/women always treat me badly
- People should respect me
- People are judging me
- I am not good enough

· I have to work hard
· I have to work two jobs to make ends meet
· My body should be healthy
· Things never work out for me
· My boss betrayed me
· I am worthless
· There is not enough time
· No pain, no gain
· I need to be in control
· People are not trustworthy
· Women should not be so emotional
· There should not be war in this world
· It's my job to make others happy
· I need more money
· I have no luck

Which of those negative beliefs would you like to C H A N G E ?

*Our beliefs and our emotions have to be a match
in order to support the manifestation of our desires.
The emotion of 'I feel worthy'
needs a matching positive belief
such as 'I AM Worthy.'*

Positive Core Beliefs That You Can
Choose to Integrate Today

· I am always loved and lovable
· My life is guided in the right direction
· No matter what challenges I encounter, I always find a way to
  overcome them
· I am a creative "Genius"
· I am experiencing huge abundance in all areas of my life
· Everything always works out for me
· I am the creator of my reality
· My body is beautiful
· I am unlimited in what I can do
· I am free
· I am an empowered being
· Other people are mirrors of myself
· People love being around me
· I trust life, I trust myself, I trust others
· I have so much prosperity in my life
· My life is successful
· I love money
· I am worthy
· My body is a healing vessel
· Everything I touch turns to gold
· My body responds to my loving commands
· I have the best job in the whole world
· I love my life
· Everything is about experience
· I always have everything I need
· I have the power to choose what is right for me in the present
  moment

If you have not, up until now,
taken a look at what you firmly believe,
then make sure it is positive,
because more than likely
you are still being run by your old programming.

Which of these positive beliefs would you like to adopt?

Can you list any of your own positive beliefs?

Choose positive beliefs that resonate with you, based on where you are today. Then, stand up for what you believe in, based on your choices and your truth. When changing beliefs, remember that they are repetitive thoughts which you think over and over again. So keep them simple and practice a few at a time until you have them grounded into your body and experience.

Making your beliefs a conscious practice is an
act of the peaceful warrior.

Now that you've revealed your inner garden to yourself, it's time to manifest it into the physical and begin your peace practice. On your journey to peace and empowerment, you are building a solid foundation that starts within. Peace is an inside job.

- I love myself
- I think positive thoughts
- I feel and release all my negative feelings
- I heal all my emotional core wounds from the past
- I expose and change my limiting beliefs to positive beliefs that are in alignment with my truth
- I live and embody my core values

What does Peace mean to YOU?

I want you to live into and reflect on the question: "What does Peace mean to you?"

Later, throughout 'The 21-Day Peace Practice', pretend you are walking a labyrinth, also asking yourself this question: "What does peace mean to me.?"

For now, write what peace means to you today:

Short Three-Step Peace Process

This short three-step process was founded by Sarah Hartzell.

Picture a time in your life when you were at peace with the world and also with yourself. Where were you, what did it feel like, what sensations did you have? Bring that vibration into your whole being now.
Say: *"I feel peaceful when........"*

What current situation or relationship is challenging you? What is it that needs to be acknowledged here?
Say: *"Peace for me in this situation would be........"*

Pledge one decisive action for the coming week in relation to the challenge.
Say: *"In the name of peace, I will........"*

The Peace Practice

Preparing For The Next 21 Days

Okay, you're almost ready to begin 'The 21-Day Practice.' Read the following information, set your beginning date, and plan your schedule for the next 21 days. You will need extra time in the morning to practice. Allow yourself one hour for the breathing, meditation and reflection. Begin your day by saying your positive affirmations—which are now becoming beliefs. You deserve this time.

As you begin going through each day's practice and meditation I want you to remember that you are being asked to get really clear with yourself.

You are being asked to speak words out loud. There is a reason for this. When you speak positive words out loud, parts within yourself which are not in resonance will come out and make themselves known. You may begin to do a lot of yawning. This is suppressed energy being released from your body. This is a great thing. You may notice that you begin to get very emotional when you are speaking the positive words out loud. This is also great. You are clearing dense energy out of your body. You may also notice that there are times when you sound like you have a frog stuck in your throat. Pay attention to this and keep speaking as you are clearing. Your body will show you where the energy is stuck. Know that this clearing is part of the process and is very necessary.

If you have some space to take quick power naps, that is also welcomed in this process. Sometimes you might just need about 15 minutes, and afterwards you will feel refreshed again.

As you progress through the days, you will be asked to answer all the questions. Do not get overwhelmed by this process. You can answer the questions with three to four words. Also, you don't have to answer all the questions the first time around. It may be helpful to go through this '21-Day Peace Practice' more than once.

This is your opportunity to get intimate with yourself and allow yourself as much room and grace as possible.

There is no perfect way to do this. All you need is to make a commitment to your daily practice, and you will begin to love it. I so wish that I would have had something like this when I started out.

What You Can Expect In The Next Three Weeks

The first week to inner peace you will practice breathing and meditation, with a healthy dose of daily gratitude and appreciation. This will raise your energy vibration, making you feel super good. Plus, the Universe—your 'executive assistant'—will be bringing you more and more experiences into your life each day to be grateful for. In addition, you will be discovering and releasing any negative thoughts and feelings from your chakra (energy) centers. There are seven major energy centers—chakras—in the body that are vital to our health and wellbeing. Negative suppressed feelings stored in our body affect the spin of these chakras, which can result in sickness and disease. It is vital for your well being that you become really good at releasing negative feelings as part of your everyday practice.

The second week you will focus on releasing negative emotions, becoming more aware of what pulls you out of your peace. What are some of the triggers being played out by the people with whom you are in close relationship (i.e., the people at your workplace, your lover or friends)? Learn to appreciate your triggers, who and what triggers you, as perfect opportunities for you to take responsibility and claim your truth.

The third week, you will go deeper into the practice of 'the art of letting go,' getting really good at releasing more and more old suppressed feelings and thoughts that are not your truth. Everything will be coming up to the surface now as you are ready to acknowledge your truth, claiming more of your peace, your joy, and your wellbeing.

Daily Habits That Are Good For You!

Conscious Breathing

Remembering to breathe consciously is the perfect peace practice, helping you to slow down and return to the present moment. During 'The 21-Day Peace Practice' conscious breathing will be part of your everyday practice. When you begin to feel its many benefits, you will want to make conscious breathing a lifelong practice.

The present moment is where you can find inner peace: the present moment is the only place of power. It is helpful to remember the importance of conscious breathing (this cannot be overemphasized). There are many times when we are not conscious of our breath. Taking deep belly breaths is calming, centering and healing. The breath is the gift of life. There are so many benefits to breathing: releasing toxins from the body; releasing tension; relaxing the body to be open and fully receptive; breathing into emotional pain to ease it.

Breathing relaxes the mind, brings clarity,
and connects us to our heart.

Breathing Ourselves Well

Sit comfortably or lie down with your back straight. Close your eyes and focus on your breath. Inhale slowly through the nose, counting to four, drawing the breath deeply into the bottom of your lungs, feeling your abdomen slowly push out naturally. Hold for two seconds, then begin to gently breathe out for a count of four through your nose or mouth, exhaling and emptying your lungs. Allow your body to relax fully as you exhale. Set your timer and begin doing five minutes of conscious breathing twice a day, once in the morning meditation and once in the evening before bed. Deep breathing provides your body's cells with oxygen.

If the body feels tight and you are in pain, breathe into the pain slowly and deeply, then breathe out. You will discover that by breathing into your emotions, your anger, your pain, your sadness, the breath can unlock stuck energy. The power of your breath frees you up and releases the old, making space for peace and warmth and clarity. Healing starts with the breath, so bring your breath into it.
We can live without food for weeks, without water for days, but without our breath we can only live for a few minutes. Here is to breathing ourselves well! Best of all: it's free.

Journaling

Your next positive peace practice is to JOURNAL. Get yourself a college-ruled notebook, or a pretty bound journal, and start getting to know yourself on a more intimate level. You have a lot to say, so many truths to discover, a voice to express, and the best way is to get it all out on paper. You will be amazed at how much of yourself has been hidden. You will love the art of journaling as a practice of peace, self-care, love and nurturing.

For the next seven days these questions will provide stimulus for your inner growth.

- *What and who are your triggers?*
- *What are your relationships mirroring to you?*
- *What are you projecting out onto others?*
- *What energy did you release and let go of today?*

· *What area of your life do you feel you want more peace in?*
· *Would you be willing to let something fall away?*
· *What is your body communicating to you?*

The 21 Peace Practice
Week One: Day 1

∾⚬〰⚬∾

Feeling Grounded

Today is a brand new day, and the energy you bring to this day is all that matters. Imagine yourself standing in the most beautiful garden. This garden has everything you need: it is filled with the most beautiful flowers; the air is plentiful; the food is delicious; the water is so clean and pure; the sun is shining brightly. Underneath a tree, you notice a beautiful basket that has extra seeds to be planted. Knowing peace begins with you, go over and plant your seeds of peace in the garden. You are also planting seeds of gratitude into the fertile ground. These seeds are sure to grow, resulting in more and more abundance. In your garden you are planting seeds of peace and gratitude, and grounding yourself into the earth, feeling rooted and connected with your body and Mother Earth—it all begins with YOU.

> *"Let your dominant intent be to feel good, which means being playful, having fun, laughing often, and looking for reasons to appreciate and practice the art of appreciation. As you practice it, the Universe, who has been watching you practice, will give you constant opportunities to express it, so that your life just gets better and better and better." ~Abraham*

List five things on the next page for which you feel really grateful in your life right now. Feel the gratitude expanding in your body, giving you a great vibrational flow to begin your morning.

1. I am grateful for the seeds of peace I am planting
2.
3.
4.
5.

You feel called to walk over to a beautiful willow tree with a big round trunk and deep strong roots. Sit down and lean your spine against the tree. Now bring your awareness and your breath to your root chakra, located at the energy center at the base of your tailbone. Its energy is red and allows you to feel connected to your body. This chakra governs the world of survival and helps us meet our basic needs. It is the root connection to our Source. The positive vibrations of this chakra allow us to feel safe, nourished and cared for. When rooted in your first chakra, you are fully embodied, feel love for your body, and trust in yourself and the world.

Take a deep breath into your root center. Leaning into the tree, feeling fully supported, and speak the following words: "I am safe. I am love. I trust myself and others. I love my body. I nourish and take really good care of myself."

Notice any negative feelings or beliefs that may come up as you speak these words. You may notice that you are not feeling safe or firmly rooted. Notice any negative feelings or beliefs you might have around disliking your body.

What major issues have you had around feeling safe and trusting in life?

What can you do in your physical environment to nurture yourself?

Do you trust yourself and the choices you make?

Have you felt depressed or helpless?

Can you identify these feelings? When did they occur?

What has made you angry?

What have you learned about yourself today?

What are you claiming for yourself now?

What negative feelings, beliefs, or stories—that no longer serve you—are you releasing today? Write a list of these negative feelings and beliefs. Then burn that list.

As you go throughout your day, keep breathing in these words: "I trust myself to take care of myself. I have a beautiful body. I love my body and I am safe. I love my body, I am love, I am safe. I am loved and supported."

Practical tools for everyday living can be found in 'The Processing Toolbox' on page 205

Week One: Day 2

Pleasure

You feel so happy to be in your peace and gratitude garden, every time you come here. You notice there is so much lush abundance in your garden, and you feel so excited and peaceful being here. You feel amazed by the incredible beauty of the garden you are seeding. You know you are making a difference and you have begun planting more seeds of gratitude as you are noticing more and more things for which to be grateful.

List five things for which you are really grateful in your life right now, while feeling the sense of gratitude expand in your body, giving you a great beginning to your day.

1. I appreciate my body
2.
3.
4.
5.

Now—off to your favorite tree. You are beginning to form a relationship with this tree. Sit and ground yourself as you breathe deeply into your second chakra, located about two inches below your navel. This chakra's color is orange. This center governs your emotional body, your creativity, your sensuality and sexuality, and your pleasure. Leaning into your beautiful supportive tree, breathe in the following words: "I am creative. I allow my emotions without judgment. I celebrate my sexuality and claim my sensual pleasure."

Notice any negative feelings or beliefs that may come up as you speak these words.

You may notice that you are not feeling like you deserve pleasure, or you may notice that you are feeling shame around your emotions, or about your sexuality.

Do you have sexual issues that need to be resolved or healed? What are they? Name them.

What makes you feel shame when it comes to your sexuality?

What are your addictions?

What is pleasure?

What makes you angry?

What are you claiming for yourself now?

What negative feelings, beliefs, or stories—that no longer serve you—are you releasing today? Write a list of these negative feelings and beliefs. Then burn that list.

As you go throughout your day, keep speaking the words: "I claim my sensual pleasure. I embrace my creativity. I allow all of my emotions without judgment. I celebrate my body and my sexuality."

Keep a daily journal of your feelings and allow all that is not positive and loving to fall away.

Practical tools for everyday living can be found in 'The Processing Toolbox' on page 205.

Week One: Day 3

Power

You feel so joyful to be In your peace and gratitude garden, every time you come here. You feel so enlivened by the incredible beauty of the garden you are seeding. You notice there is so much lush abundance in your garden, and feel so excited and peaceful being here. By saying yes to you, and bringing your love to this garden, it is sure to grow in more and more beauty and abundance. Today you are seeding your incredible love into the fertile ground. Have you made friends with the beautiful butterflies that have the most amazing wings you have ever laid your eyes on? You have brought with you a stepping stone to reflect back to you what you value and the energy with which you are seeding your garden. On this first stone, you have painted the word 'Peace.'

List five things in your life right now for which you are really grateful. Feel the feelings of gratitude expand throughout your body, giving you a great base to begin your morning.

1. I am feeling my love for my physical body
2.
3.
4.
5.

Onward to your favorite tree. You are beginning to form a relationship with this tree, so how about giving the tree a name? Or—just listen as you lean into the incredible wisdom of this noble tree, as it whispers its name to you. Ground yourself as you breathe deeply into your third chakra, which is located three inches above your navel. This chakra color is yellow, and its balanced spin will assist you with willpower and self-direction. Feeling grounded through your breath, speak the following words: "I am confident. I love and value myself. I am powerful. I am brave. I act with clear intention and integrity in my life."

Notice any negative feelings or beliefs that may come up as you speak these words.

You may notice that you are not feeling like you are powerful or confident, or you may notice that you are feeling a lack of value or love for yourself, or you may notice where you are giving others power over you, or giving your power away. It's that nagging feeling in the pit of your stomach.

Contemplate what kind of people in your life trigger you & why?

If you reclaim your power, will you use it responsibly?

Where in your relationships do you feel victimized?

What makes you angry about that?

What are you claiming for yourself now?

What negative feelings, beliefs, or stories—that no longer serve you—are you releasing today? Write a list of these negative feelings and beliefs. Then burn that list. Be clear on what you are letting go, then affirm your choice of positive intentions.

As you go throughout your day keep speaking the words: "I am learning to set boundaries in a firm but compassionate way. I am confident in my physical body. I love and value myself. I am powerful. I am brave. I am beautiful."

Practical tools for everyday living can be found in 'The Processing Toolbox' on page 205.

Week One: Day 4

Love, Self-Love, & Forgiveness

Today is Day 4 of your visits to your peace and gratitude garden. You feel so amazed by the incredible beauty of the garden you are seeding. You notice the air is so clean —there is a feeling of calm and peace. You know by your saying yes to you, and by your saying yes to your peace, your visions, and by bringing your love to this garden, it is sure to grow in more and more beauty and abundance. Today in the garden you notice the slight wind that is caressing your skin—it feels warm and inviting, and you are excited to go see your tree. You have brought with you another stepping stone, which you carefully place, feeling much appreciation. It reads 'Gratitude.'

List five things for which you are really grateful in your life right now. Experience the feelings of gratitude expand in your body, providing you with a great start to your morning.

1. I always do the best I can. I am grateful for that
2.
3.
4.
5.

Sit with your beautiful butt against the spine of your tree and ground yourself as you breathe deeply into your fourth chakra, located along your spine, right in the center of your chest next to your physical heart. This connects you to the vibration of love, kindness, compassion and security. Place your hand over your beautiful heart and breathe deeply as you speak the following words: "I am love. I am lovable. I love with an open heart. I love myself. I forgive myself. I forgive others. I am open to the compassion of Divine Source. I have healthy loving relationships."

Notice any negative feelings or beliefs that may come up as you speak these words.

You may notice that you are not feeling like you are lovable, or you may notice that you are feeling unloved by others, or feeling that there is a sense of unworthiness, feeling not good enough.

What triggered these emotions?

Do you practice loving yourself?

Do you feel love and compassion for where you are right now?

With whom in your life do you still have unresolved issues? Name them.

Are there people in your life whom you need to forgive? Who are they, and are you ready to forgive them?

What makes you angry?

What are you claiming for yourself now?

What negative feelings, beliefs, or stories—that no longer serve you—are you releasing today? Write a list of these negative feelings and beliefs. Then burn that list. Release everything and surrender the past.

As you go throughout your day keep speaking the words: "I am love. I am lovable. I love with an open heart. I love myself. I forgive myself. I forgive others. I am open to the compassion of Divine Source. I have healthy, loving relationships."

Self Forgiveness Mantra
"I forgive myself, I forgive myself, I forgive myself, I forgive myself, I forgive myself, I forgive myself." All day long, baby.

Forgiveness Exercise
Sit and ask your angels and guides to be with you.
Open all the doors of your heart. Invite into your heart the ones who have hurt you, and tell them you forgive them for what caused you pain.

Practical tools for everyday living can be found in 'The Processing Toolbox' on page 205.

Week One: Day 5

Communication

It is Day 5 of your visits to your peace and gratitude garden. "I am Peace. Peace is in me." You are feeling so much appreciation for the incredible magic of the garden you are seeding. You notice there is beauty in abundance, and that you are making a difference by your visits, adding your incredible charm to the most enchanted and peaceful garden on earth. The sun is just rising, greeting you with a big glorious smile, and you feel like the sun said to you, "Good Morning Sunshine, how are you?"

List five things that you are really grateful for in your life right now. Feel the feelings of gratitude expand throughout your body, giving you a great start to your morning. Really feel the sensations fully in your body.

1. I am grateful for my courage
2.
3.
4.
5.

As you joyfully sit snugly against your very old friend, and you breathe and ground yourself into your body, breathe into your fifth center, the throat chakra. Sky blue in color and located at the base of the throat, this chakra governs the true meaning of communication, psychic consciousness, speaking, hearing and listening: listening to the wisdom of your soul. Breathe in and speak the following words: "I joyfully speak my truth. I express myself with clarity and courage.

I joyfully share my creative gifts with the world. I communicate easily. I listen deeply to the wisdom of my soul. I am authentic in my expression."

Notice any negative feelings or beliefs that may come up as you speak these words.

You may notice that you are not feeling like you are able to express yourself well, or you may feel afraid to speak up and speak your truth, or you may be feeling like you are not heard, that nobody listens to you.

Do you have difficulty in speaking? What hinders you from expressing yourself to people who trigger you?

Do you find yourself not saying something, and later wishing you had done so?

What makes you angry about that?

Do you use negative language to express yourself?

How do you communicate with your family, boss or your partner?

Are there areas in your communication where you are letting things slide, or turning a blind eye?

What are you claiming for yourself now?

What negative feelings, beliefs, or stories—that no longer serve you—are you releasing today? Write the list of the negative feelings, and do your daily ritual of burning the old suppressed feelings, habits, beliefs and thoughts that are not positive.

As you go throughout your day, count the times you speak power-fully, non-apologetically.

Also, keep speaking the words: "I joyfully speak my truth. I express myself with clarity and courage. I joyfully share my creative gifts with the world. I communicate easily. I listen deeply to the wisdom of my soul. I am authentic."

Practical tools for everyday living can be found in 'The Processing Toolbox' on page 205.

Week One: Day 6

Intuition

Today is Day 6 of seeding your peace and gratitude garden. Here comes the sun, little darling. You feel so excited as you return to your peace and gratitude garden. This is the place where miracles happen. There is so much love, beauty and abundance. Your own Heaven on Earth, this is the place where you get to bring your best self, your happy self, your peaceful self, knowing that here all is well.

Everyday you see something new that you have not seen before. You feel so much appreciation for your life and the part you are playing in bringing peace to the Earth. You did not realize it could be that simple, and you did not know that it would make such a difference in your life and in all of the lives you touch. You joyfully start skipping, taking your first step onto your peace stone, feeling so thankful for peace in your present moment. Then step onto your 'Gratitude' stone, feeling so much appreciation for this short amount of time, as you notice so much has already improved in the last six days of your life.

You love focusing on more things to appreciate today, so let's appreciate more things about YOU: feel good, feel happy, feel healthy, feel loved, feel abundant, feel creative, feel compassionate, feel knowledgeable, feel powerful.

List five things for which you are really grateful in your life right now. Feel the feelings of appreciation expand in your body, giving you a great start to begin your morning.

1. You appreciate your ability to feel—to feel your feelings
2.
3.
4.
5.

As you connect with your tree, you realize this way of grounding every day is really helping you feel connected to the earth. You feel your roots extending deep into the earth, as you breathe and ground yourself into your body. Breathe into your sixth center, called the third-eye chakra. Deep indigo blue in color, it is located in the center of your forehead. This chakra, also known as your vision center, governs the power of imagination and intuition. A harmonious sixth chakra will assist you in bringing your vision and your true nature into harmony with your Spirit. Breathe in, and speak the following words: "I SEE. I honor my crystal clear insight. I am open to the powerful magic of my imagination. I claim my intuitive knowing. I create beautiful dreams, beginning with my peace and gratitude garden. I am a visionary."

Notice any negative feelings or beliefs that may come up as you speak these words.

You may notice old feelings coming up, revealing your distrust in your intuition. Maybe you had bad dreams as a child, and couldn't remember these dreams. Perhaps you feel you don't have much of an imagination.

Have you had bad dreams or good dreams that you remember?

Do you attempt to learn the meaning of them, wondering what your subconscious and superconscious minds are communicating to you?

Do you dream the same dream over and over again? If so, what do you think it means?

How many times have you intuited something, like knowing who was calling you, or knowing you felt guided to call someone and they were just thinking of you? How many times have you just passed that off as 'weird'?

What is intuition?

What brings up anger for you?

What are you claiming for yourself now?

What negative feelings, beliefs, or stories —that no longer serve you—are you releasing today? Breathe in and allow yourself to feel, without judgment, any beliefs that may arise. Are you ready to release them? Make your list of negative feelings that you are releasing, letting go of all negative thoughts. Burn your list. Now you are choosing positive loving thoughts.

Breathe in and speak the following words: "I SEE. I honor my crystal clear insight. I am open to the powerful magic of my imagination. I claim my intuitive knowing. I create beautiful dreams, beginning with my peace and gratitude garden. I am a visionary."

Practical tools for everyday living can be found in 'The Processing Toolbox' on page 205.

Week One: Day 7

Your Connection to Source

It is Day 7 of your visits to your peace and gratitude garden. How does your body feel as you enter your peace and gratitude garden? Is your imagination soaring with all kinds of new ideas and inspiration? You have cultivated a sacred space for yourself, which you are seeding from your very own peaceful inner center. On this very special day you have brought with you another stepping stone on which you will paint another sacred word, seeding your garden with *'Compassion'*—for yourself and for all the people in the world.

List five things that you are really grateful for in your life right now. Feel the feelings of gratitude expand in your body, giving you a great basis for beginning your morning. *What is your optimal feeling?*

1. I AM so grateful for my Compassionate Heart
2.
3.
4.
5.

Here you are hugging your tree, feeling so grateful. This grounding ritual every day is really helping you feel connected to the earth. You feel your roots extending deep into the earth as you breathe and ground yourself into your body. Now breathe into your seventh chakra, located at the highest point of your body—the crown of your head. This chakra is connected to your pineal gland, its color is violet, and it governs the consciousness of spiritual awakening, inner wisdom, and the gifts of enlightenment.

Breathe and speak the following words: "I am united. I am grateful. I am deeply connected to Spirit. I am one with the Divine. Bliss awakens within my heart, body and soul."

Notice any negative feelings or beliefs that may come up as you speak these words.

You may notice old feelings that make you afraid to express your authentic spiritual beliefs, or beliefs that suggest to you that you are separate from your Divine Source.

What about beliefs that result in feeling isolated from life, or feeling alone?

Do you have any negative thoughts about your connection to the Divine Source?

How do you feel about your relationship to the Divine Source or God?

Do you feel isolated from Life?

Does this bring up anger for you?

Do you feel at peace with your spirituality?

What are you claiming for yourself now?

What negative feelings, beliefs, or stories—that no longer serve you—are you releasing today? Breathe in and allow yourself to feel for a moment (without judgment) any beliefs that may arise. Are you ready to release and let go of those that no longer serve you? Make your list of negative feelings. You are releasing and letting go of all negative thoughts. Burn your list. You are choosing positive loving thoughts only.

Breathe and speak the following words throughout your day: "I am united with all that is. I am grateful. I am Peaceful. I am deeply connected to Spirit. I am one with the Divine, and bliss awakens within my heart, body and soul."

Congratulations for seeding your peace and gratitude garden—you have been coming here for seven days! Now we will continue on for the next seven days, choosing to be in peace with all that is going on in your life and within you.

Practical tools for everyday living can be found in 'The Processing Toolbox' on page 205.

The 21 Peace Practice
Week Two: Day 8

———∞⃝∞———

Honoring Yourself

This week you will be releasing negative emotions, becoming more aware of what takes you out of your peace. Who and what are some of the triggers being played out by the people with whom you are in close relationship: the people at your workplace; your lover; friends?

Learn to appreciate your triggers—who and what triggers you—as perfect opportunities for you to take responsibility and claim your truth. So far we have had seven days and seven chakras to celebrate and appreciate.

For the next seven days these are your growth opportunities:
- *Who and what are your triggers?*
- *What do relationships mirror to you?*
- *What energy did you release and let go of today?*
- *In what areas of your life do you want more peace?*
- *Would you be willing to let something fall away?*
- *What is your body communicating to you?*

It is Day 8 of your creation in your peace and gratitude garden. How does your body feel with all the love and gratitude you are bringing into your sacred space? In your process of releasing all that is not true, you are making room for more light, love, and peace to enter into that space. You are here to shine your brilliant light and bring the unique expression that only you can bring. You are here to create the New Earth, to be your greatest self, and live fearlessly. What does the New Earth look like to you? What does it feel like? The most important practice is 'Self-Love.' Joyfully grab and plant the seeds of self-love into the fertile ground, and be sure to cultivate this most sacred relationship with yourself as you grow in abundance with your daily attention to nurturing yourself. And—place another stepping stone in your garden with 'Self-Love' written on the stone.

List five things for which you are really grateful in your life right now. Feel the feelings of gratitude expand in your body, giving you a great beginning to your day. Expand the feelings of appreciation out to everyone you see.

1. I deeply love myself; I am so grateful to be me
2.
3.
4.
5.

With your eyes open, breathe deeply into your root center. Breathe into this first center, the root chakra, while leaning into the tree, feeling fully supported, and breathe the following words into your body: "I am safe. I am love. I am loving myself. I love myself. I trust myself and others. I love my body. I nourish and take really good care of myself."

Notice any negative feelings or beliefs that may come up as you speak these words.

Loving yourself starts with you. Speaking the above words, what does not feel true to you?

What are some of the changes you would like to make that would be more honoring to yourself?

Where do you limit yourself?

What do you allow in your relationships that makes you feel not good enough?

What makes you angry about that?

What is underneath that anger that you want to claim as your truth? (Remember, when you release feelings of powerlessness, you claim your power.)

What negative feelings, beliefs, or stories—that no longer serve you—are you releasing today? Write the list of the negative feelings, and do your daily ritual of burning the list of old suppressed feelings, habits, beliefs, and thoughts that are not positive.

What in your life do you want to claim more of?

What action step and commitment will you make today toward practicing the principles of self-love and self-care?

I affirm: "I act this way because I deeply value myself."

Keep breathing and repeating the words: "I am lovable. I love, honor, and approve of myself. I deeply value myself. I deeply love myself. I deeply honor my body and myself."

Practical tools for everyday living can be found in 'The Processing Toolbox' on page 205.

Week Two: Day 9

Prosperity

Today is the 9th day of seeding your peace and gratitude garden. You bring with you another stepping stone, and before you paint the word 'Prosperity' on it, take your seeds and plant them in your beautiful garden. You deserve all the prosperity and all the wealth you desire to live an abundant life. You know the past is past and you are now claiming your Divine birthright. As a magnificent, exceptional being, you fully deserve to live a joyous life filled with vibrant health, love, and financial well being. You are worthy of nothing less!

List five things for which you are really grateful in your life right now. Feel the feelings of gratitude expand throughout your body, giving you a great vibrational flow with which to begin your morning.

1. I always have everything that I need
2.
3.
4.
5.

Now, at your favorite willow tree, sit and ground yourself as you breathe deeply into your second chakra, located about two inches beneath your navel. This chakra's color is orange, and governs your emotional body, your sensuality and sexuality, your creativity, and your pleasure. Leaning into your beautiful supportive tree, breathe in the following words: "I am creative. I allow my emotions to rise without judgment. I celebrate my sexuality and claim my sensual pleasure."

Notice any negative feelings or beliefs that may come up as you speak these words.

You may notice that you are not feeling as if you deserve pleasure, or you may notice that you are feeling shame around your emotions or your sexuality.

How do you like to express your creativity?

What are some of the creative projects to which you would like to give birth?

How do you express your emotions? Are you able to express them fully? What do you do when your buttons get pushed?

What does pleasure mean to YOU?

What can you claim more of in your life today in order to celebrate your sexuality and sensuality more?

What negative feelings, beliefs, or stories—that no longer serve you—are you releasing today? What feelings and thoughts are you writing on your list that you are burning?

Throughout your day, keep breathing and speaking the words: "I am Creative. I embrace all of my emotions without judgment. I am sexually alive, and I love feeling pleasure. I deserve to feel all of my feelings fully. I claim my sexual pleasure. I love me."

Practical tools for everyday living can be found in 'The Processing Toolbox' on page 205.

Week Two: Day 10

Trust & Confidence

Here you are again in your peace and gratitude garden, feeling happy, feeling alive, feeling at peace—bringing your consciousness into your garden, seeding it with love and your daily focus of appreciation. There is so much beauty present. *What is your favorite nature experience? When do you feel most at harmony while in nature?*

On this very special day, you brought along another important stepping stone on which you will paint your sacred word 'Trust.' But, before you paint your new word onto the stone, grab some seeds from your seed basket and place your seeds, infused with the intention of trust, into the fertile ground. Trust that the seeds you are planting will bear fruit: trusting yourself; trusting others; trusting life; trusting the Divine.

List five things that you are really grateful for in your life right now. Feel the feelings of gratitude expand throughout your body, giving you a great vibrational flow with which to begin your morning.

1. I always make the right choice, and take the right action
2.
3.
4.
5.

Ground yourself as you breathe deeply into your third chakra, located three inches above your navel. This chakra color is yellow, and its harmonious spin will assist you with willpower and self-direction. Feeling grounded, breathe deeply, and on the exhale speak the following words: "I am confident. I love and value myself. I am powerful. I am brave. I act with clear intention and integrity in my life."

Notice any negative feelings or beliefs that may come up as you speak these words.

In what area of your life would you like to claim more power: your finances; your physical body; your relationships; your career?

Where do you give your power away? To whom and when?

What is your contribution to the world going to be?

What have you wanted to do, and have not yet done?

What keeps you from winning?

List your justifications.

List your expectations.

In releasing and letting go of so many old feelings and beliefs, we are always investigating our integrity. What does integrity mean to you? Where would you like to see yourself being more in integrity in your life?

Are you willing to release the victim and reclaim your power? Will you use it responsibly?

What negative feelings, beliefs, or stories—that no longer serve you—are you releasing today? Make your list and burn it, then watch your life change.

Be clear on what you are letting go, then affirm your choice of positive intentions.

As you proceed throughout your day, continue to hold your intention to be in integrity and keep repeating the words: "I am true to myself. I am confident. I feel confident. I choose to be confident. I am powerful. I feel powerful. I choose to be in my power. I love myself. I feel my love, and I choose my love. I embrace my power in a loving way."

Practical tools for everyday living can be found in 'The Processing Toolbox' on page 205.

Week Two: Day 11

───❦───

Beauty, Acceptance, & Your Heart's Desire

I t is Day 11 of your visit to your peace and gratitude garden. Affirm: "I am peace, peace is in me. I am joy, joy is in me. I am love, love is in me."

You are feeling so much appreciation for the incredible beauty in the garden you have been seeding. There is so much enchantment being created by your visits, your daily focus, and by your commitment. You are making a difference, adding your own incredible magic to the most beautiful, peaceful garden on earth—from the inside out. Thank you so much for taking the time to honor your practice. Remember to be gentle with yourself, as you are experiencing enormous change. There is so much to accept, and this is the perfect time to plant seeds of acceptance everywhere. Acceptance is such a powerful word. It is perfect to place the stone 'Acceptance' in your garden now. With all the change that is happening, no matter what it might be, saying the words 'I accept' will support you immediately, releasing resistance to what is. Repeat: "I accept. I accept. I accept."

List five things for which you are really grateful in your life right now. Feel the feelings of gratitude expand in your body, giving you a great vibrational flow to begin your morning.

1. I accept and approve of myself
2.
3.
4.
5.

Grounding and breathing into your fourth chakra (located at the center of your heart) connects you to the vibration of love, kindness, compassion, and security. Place your hand over your beautiful heart and breathe deeply as you speak the following words: "I am love. I am lovable. I love with an open heart. I love myself. I forgive myself. I forgive others. I am open to the compassion of Divine Source. I have healthy loving relationships. I love my body. I love my life."

Notice any negative feelings or beliefs that may come up as you speak these words.

Listening to your heart is one of the most loving acts of self-love. What is your heart's desire?

Are you willing to let your heart lead you?

What is your heart communicating to you? Are you listening?

What is it to love deeply?

What deeply motivates me?

Who am I becoming?

Where are you holding yourself back from experiencing more love?

What would you like to acknowledge about yourself?

Do you feel lovable? Do you feel safe? What triggers these emotions?

What negative feelings, beliefs, or stories—that no longer serve you—are you releasing today? Write a list of the negative feelings and do your daily ritual of burning the list of old suppressed feelings, habits, beliefs, and thoughts that are not positive.

Self forgiveness mantra: "I forgive myself, I forgive myself, I forgive myself, I forgive myself, I forgive myself, I forgive myself."

As you go through your day, keep affirming and speaking the following words: "I am love. I am lovable. I love with an open heart. I love myself. I forgive myself. I forgive others. I am open to the compassion of Divine Source. I have healthy, loving relationships. I love my body. I love my life. I love myself."

Practical tools for everyday living can be found in 'The Processing Toolbox' on page 205.

Week Two: Day 12

Speaking from your Heart

Forgive yourself every day—for everything. Gandhi said, "Be the change you wish to see in the world." It is time for you to be the peace you want to see in the world. Be the love you want to see in the world. Be the passion you want to see in the world. Your thoughts, emotions, and feelings are a huge contribution to this planet. You came here to experience peace on Earth, and so you shall. Peace is an inside job, and takes daily practice and responsibility to do your part. Here in your peace and gratitude garden, notice how much there is for which to be grateful. What is the dominant spirit of how you want to feel? Expand and connect to that feeling all day long: "I choose joy, I choose well-being, I choose passion." Plant seeds of 'Passion' into your garden today, and place your stone with love and care as you skip passionately into your day. What are you really passionate about?

List five things you are really grateful for in your life right now. Feel and connect to those feelings as gratitude expands in your body, giving you a great vibrational flow to begin your morning.

1. I am so grateful for my passion
2.
3.
4.
5.

Leaning into your tree, breathe and ground yourself into your body, while you breathe into your fifth center. This is the throat chakra, sky blue in color, located at the level of the throat. It controls the true meaning of communication, psychic consciousness, hearing, speaking, and listening—listening to the wisdom of your soul. Breathe in and speak the following words: "I joyfully speak my truth. I express myself with clarity and courage. I joyfully share my creative gifts with the world. I communicate easily. I listen deeply to the wisdom of my soul. I am authentic."

Notice any negative feelings or beliefs that may come up as you speak these words.

You may notice that you are not feeling like you express yourself well, or you may feel afraid to speak up and speak your truth, or you may be feeling like you are not heard and nobody listens to you.

What is it to speak and act from your heart?

Where have you denied yourself—and others?

Do you feel safe expressing your true self?

How do you sabotage yourself?

Where do you fall short?

What is it you should give yourself permission to do today?

What are you claiming for yourself now?

Do you hold back, not saying something out of fear that you may be hurting someone if you do speak your truth? If so, what makes you angry about that?

What negative feelings or habits are you releasing today that no longer serve you? Write the list of negative feelings, and do your daily ritual of burning the old suppressed feelings, habits, beliefs, and thoughts that are not positive.

As you go throughout your day keep speaking the words: "I joyfully speak my truth with love and kindness. I express myself with clarity and courage. I joyfully share my creative gifts with the world. I communicate easily. I listen deeply to the wisdom of my soul. I am authentic."

Practical tools for everyday living can be found in 'The Processing Toolbox' on page 205.

Week Two: Day 13

Fun & Inner Visions

Today is the 13th day of seeding your peace and gratitude garden. Aren't you loving this inner garden that you have been cultivating with so much care and beauty? Look around and you see the most colorful flowers everywhere. These favorite flowers make you so happy. Your body is feeling relaxed and receptive.

Today you have brought a swing with you to hang from your tree, so that you can swing like you did when you were a kid. You sit on your very own swing, feeling so much appreciation for your new sacred space—the space that now lives in your heart forever. You never realized that letting go of old feelings, old thoughts, and old energy could be healing you! You are so happy being in this space where all the love you are is joyfully reflected back to you in so many beautiful ways. You find that this is the perfect time to plant seeds of fun, and of course to place a beautiful stepping stone—'Fun'—into your garden. It reminds you to allow your inner child to come out and play.

List five things that you are really grateful for in your life right now. Feel the feelings of gratitude expand throughout your body, giving you a great vibrational flow to begin your morning.

1. All my bills are paid
2.
3.
4.
5.

Breathe and ground yourself into your body. Place your awareness on your sixth center and breathe into this 'third eye' chakra, deep indigo blue in color, located at the center of your forehead. This chakra governs your imagination, and is also known as your inner vision and intuition center. The positive spin here will help you live in peace and harmony, as you bring your inner vision and your true nature into harmony with your spirit.

Breathe in and speak the following words: "I SEE, and I honor my crystal clear insight. I am open to the powerful magic of my imagination. I claim my intuitive knowing. I create beautiful dreams beginning in my peace and gratitude garden. I am a visionary."

Notice any negative feelings or beliefs that may come up as you speak these words.

You may not resonate with all of the spoken words, and some emotions might arise for you. They are showing you what areas in your life deeply want to be acknowledged.

"Imagination is more important than knowledge." ~Albert Einstein

Was your imagination honored when you were a child?

Do you spend time imagining new ways of living your life?

What powerful questions can you ask yourself each morning?

What does it mean 'to be intuitive'?

What are some of the clear insights you have gotten in the past? List some and name them.

If you were at your best right now, what would you do?

What is does it mean to you 'to be complete'?

Do you practice any meditative techniques such as walking, breathing, guided meditations, silent meditations?

What negative feelings, beliefs, or stories—that no longer serve you—are you releasing today? Breathe in and allow yourself to feel for a moment (without judgment) any beliefs that may arise. Are you ready to release and let go of those old beliefs that no longer serve you? Make your list of negative feelings to release, letting go of all your negative thoughts. Burn your list. You are choosing positive, loving thoughts only.

Breathe in and speak the following words as you go throughout your day: "I choose to see, and I honor my insight. I am open to the powerful magic of my imagination. I claim my intuitive knowing. I create beautiful dreams, beginning with my peace and gratitude garden. I am a visionary."

Practical tools for everyday living can be found in 'The Processing Toolbox' on page 205.

Week Two: Day 14

Feeling Connected to Source

This is Day 14 of your visits to your peace and gratitude garden. Your imagination is soaring with all kinds of new ideas and inspirations. You are learning to value your sense of peace and your desire for solitude by starting off your day by bringing your attention to all the things for which you are grateful. When you reflect upon all the gifts in your life, and you really take a look at how much abundance there is, giving thanks and blessing it all will increase your vibration and your inner feeling of JOY. Feeling grateful and thankful for everything—including those things that challenge you—is helping you grow.

When you find gratitude for everything in your life, you step away from victimization and move into empowerment and appreciation.

List five things in your life right now for which you are really grateful. Feel the feelings of gratitude expand throughout your body, giving you a great foundation to begin your morning. What is your dominant feeling of choice today?

1. I have so much appreciation for all the angels on my team
2.
3.
4.
5.

Here you are hugging your tree, feeling so grateful. The daily practice of grounding is really helping you feel connected to the earth.

Once again, feel your roots extending deep into the earth as you breathe and ground yourself into your body. Now breathe into your seventh chakra, located at the highest point of your body, the crown of your head. This chakra governs the consciousness of spiritual awakening, inner wisdom, and the gifts of enlightenment. This chakra is connected to your pineal gland and its color is violet.

Speak the following words: "I am united with all that is. I am grateful. I am deeply connected to Spirit, and I am one with the Divine. Bliss awakens within my heart."

Notice any negative feelings or beliefs that may come up as you speak these words.

You may notice old feelings coming up that make you feel afraid to express your authentic spiritual beliefs: beliefs of feeling isolated from life; beliefs that suggest that you are separate from the Divine Source.

What does it mean to be exceptional?

How have you withheld yourself from life?

Do you feel connected to Source and your angelic team?

What do you feel awakening in your heart?

How does it feel to be in awe?

What is it like to be generous with yourself?

What are you claiming for yourself now?

What negative feelings or beliefs or stories that no longer serve you are you releasing today? Breathe in and allow yourself, without judgment, to feel for a moment any beliefs that may arise. Are you ready to release and let go of those that no longer serve you? Make your list of the negative feelings you are releasing. Burn your list. You are letting go of all those negative thoughts. You are choosing positive, loving thoughts only.

Breathe and speak the following words throughout your day: "I am united with all that is. I am grateful. I am peaceful. I am deeply connected to Spirit. I am one with the Divine. Bliss awakens within my heart."

Practical tools for everyday living can be found in 'The Processing Toolbox' on page 205.

The 21 Peace Practice
Week Three: Day 15

$$\infty\!\sim\!\infty$$

Feeling Worthy

You will now go more deeply into the practice of 'the art of letting go.' You are getting really good at releasing more and more old suppressed feelings and thoughts that are not your own truth. Everything's coming up to the surface now as you are ready to acknowledge your truth, claiming more of your peace, your joy, and your well-being.

For the next seven days these are your growth opportunities for liberation:

> · *What and who are your triggers?*
> · *What are your relationships mirroring to you?*
> · *What energy did you release and let go of today?*
> · *In which areas of your life do you desire more peace?*
> · *Would you be willing to let something fall away?*
> · *What is your body communicating to you?*

This is Day 15 of creating your peace and gratitude garden. You bring with you another stepping stone, and before you paint the word 'worthy' on it, grab your seeds and plant these worthy seeds into your beautiful garden. You deserve all the prosperity and all the wealth you desire to live an abundant life.

In your evolution of releasing all that is not true, you are creating space for more light, love and peace. You are choosing peace as your ally, establishing peace in your life, in your finances, and through making peace with your past and present, you are bringing peace into your future.

List five things that you are really grateful for in your life right now. Feel the feelings of gratitude expand throughout your body, giving you a great beginning to your day. Expand your feelings of appreciation out to everyone you see.

1. I deeply trust myself. It's an honor to be me
2.
3.
4.
5.

With your eyes open, take a deep breath into your root center. Breathe into your base chakra, leaning into your tree, feeling fully supported, breathe the following words into your body: "I am safe. I am love. I am loving myself. I love myself. I trust myself and others. I love my body. I nourish and take really good care of myself."

Notice any negative feelings or beliefs that may come up as you speak these words.

> Take a look at the places outside of yourself where you are seeking love or approval from someone. First and foremost, do you approve of yourself?

> What is abundance?

What do you deeply value about yourself?

How is that reflected in your relationships?

What is your closest relationship mirroring to you?

Are there any triggers about that?

Where are you holding yourself back?

What is underneath that anger that you want to claim as your truth? Remember, when we release feelings of powerlessness, we claim our power.

What negative feelings, beliefs, or stories—that no longer serve you—are you releasing today? Write the list of negative feelings and do your daily ritual of burning the list of old suppressed feelings, habits, beliefs, and thoughts that are not positive.

What more in your life are you wanting to claim?

Because you deeply value yourself, you keep breathing and repeating these words: "I am so loveable. I love, honor, and approve of myself. I deeply value myself. I deeply love myself. I deeply honor my body and myself."

Practical tools for everyday living can be found in 'The Processing Toolbox' on page 205.

Week Three: Day 16

Truth & Sexuality

It is Day 16 of seeding your peace and gratitude garden. You have brought with you another stepping stone, and before you paint the word 'Truth,' plant the seeds of truth into your beautiful garden. You are here to be your authentic self, your true Divine nature. Standing in your truth takes courage. You are releasing so many emotions, beliefs, habits, and patterns, allowing you to progress deeper into your truth. When you are not in integrity, you will feel a nagging inside, telling you something is off and you are out of alignment. When you are in integrity with yourself, you will feel peaceful, assured that clarity of your truth will be the next step to take. Being at peace means living your truth.

List five things for which you are really grateful for in your life right now. Feel the feelings of gratitude expand throughout your body, giving you a great vibrational flow to begin your morning.

1. I heal through the power of Gratitude
2.
3.
4.
5.

Now at to your favorite tree, sit and ground yourself as you breathe deeply into your second chakra (located beneath your belly button, about two inches from your navel). This chakra governs your emotional body, your sensuality and sexuality, your creativity, and your pleasure. Its color is orange. Leaning into your beautiful supportive tree, breathe in the following words: "I am creative. I allow my emotions without judgment. I celebrate my sexuality and claim my sensual pleasure."

Notice any negative feelings or beliefs that may come up as you speak these words. You may notice that you are feeling like you do not deserve pleasure, or you may notice that you are feeling shame around your emotions or your sexuality.

Did you experience sexual abuse as a child?

Is there still healing that needs to happen there?

Do you experience any compulsive behavior that you cannot control?

What are some of the steps that you can take to change that behavior?

If you could create and do anything, what would that be? What negative feelings, beliefs, or stories—that no longer serve you—are you releasing today? What feelings and thoughts are you writing on your list that you will burn?

As you go throughout your day, keep breathing and speaking the words: "I am creative. I embrace all of my emotions without judgment. I am sexually alive. I love feeling pleasure. I deserve to feel all of my feelings fully. I claim my sexual pleasure. I love me."

Practical tools for everyday living can be found in 'The Processing Toolbox' on page 205.

Week Three: Day 17

Empowerment

Today is Day 17 of seeding your peace and gratitude garden. You are even more committed to Being yourself, and celebrating yourself. How amazingly loving, talented, and brilliant you are! Today is the best day of your life and you are celebrating YOU. There is not anything that you can not do. You came here to live your best life and bring your laughter and your joy to your relationships. As you dance your way through your garden today, allow your dominant feeling to be playful, feeling good, looking for beauty everywhere, looking for reasons to appreciate and practice the art of appreciation. You joyfully plant more seeds today, along with another stepping stone: 'Empowerment.' Planting seeds of empowerment, while releasing your anger and powerlessness, is part of your claiming your truth.

List five things for which you are really grateful in your life right now. Feel the feelings of gratitude expand throughout your body, giving you a great vibrational flow with which to begin your morning.

1. I am grateful, and I feel powerful!
2.
3.
4.
5.

Ground yourself, as you breathe deeply into your third chakra, located three inches above your navel. This chakra's color is yellow, and balanced, its spin will assist you with willpower and self-direction. Feeling grounded, take a deep breath and speak the following words: "I am confident. I love and value myself. I am powerful. I am brave. I act with clear intention and integrity in my life."

Notice any negative feelings or beliefs that may come up as you speak these words.

What about power struggles? There might be a challenge with an authority figure, or with anyone to whom you give your power away. This powerlessness can feel like a sharp pain in your solar plexus.

Do you feel powerless in some situations? Name them.

What do you project onto your partners or close relationships that leaves you feeling the victim?

What would be a more response-able action to take?

What are some of the changes you would like to make that would be more honoring for you? Remember, when we release the feelings of powerlessness, we claim our power.

What is a decision you have been avoiding?

Where might you be in denial?

What negative feelings, beliefs, or stories—that no longer serve you—are you releasing today? Make your list, then burn it, and watch your life change.

Be clear about what you are releasing, then affirm your choice of positive intentions. As you go throughout your day, set your intention to stay in your integrity. Keep repeating the words: "I am confident. I feel confident. I choose to be confident. I am powerful. I feel powerful. I choose to be in my power. I love myself. I feel my love. I choose to be love. I AM."

Practical tools for everyday living can be found in 'The Processing Toolbox' on page 205.

Week Three: Day 18

Commitment

It is Day 18 of your visits to your peace and gratitude garden. "I am peace, peace is in me. I am joy, joy is in me. I am love, love is in me." You are feeling so much appreciation from the incredible beauty of the garden you have been seeding. You experience much beauty through your visits, your daily focus and your commitment. You are making a difference, adding your incredible beauty to this most beautiful, peaceful garden on earth. Today you are seeding your garden with commitment to yourself. It is about giving your word to yourself and keeping it. Committing to yourself should always be your highest priority. Know that your commitments will support your evolution and your growth. Place your stone of 'Commitment' into your garden, allow the sacred ritual to be honoring of your word.

List five things that you are really grateful for in your life right now. Feel the feelings of gratitude expand throughout your body, giving you a great vibrational flow with which to begin your morning.

1. I am in harmony within
2.
3.
4.
5.

Grounding and breathing into your fourth chakra (located at the center of your heart) connects you to the vibration of love, kindness, compassion, and security. Place your hand over your beautiful heart, and breathe deeply as you speak the following words: "I am love. I am lovable. I love with an open heart. I love myself. I forgive myself. I forgive others. I am open to the compassion of the Divine Source. I have healthy, loving relationships. I love my body. I love my life."

Do you notice any negative feelings or beliefs that may come up as you speak these words?

What does the word 'commitment' mean to you?

What is out of alignment in your life?

Are there any unresolved feelings about past relationships that still weigh heavily on you?

Are you able to move out of the victim mode and move into the awareness that each person, situation, and event offers us a gift of learning, love, and forgiveness?

What is your heart communicating to you. Are you listening?

Are there persons in your life whom you need to forgive, letting them, and you, off the hook?

What negative feelings, beliefs, or stories—that no longer serve you—are you releasing today? Write the list of negative feelings and do your daily ritual of burning the list of old suppressed feelings, habits, beliefs, and thoughts that are not positive.

Self-forgiveness mantra: "I forgive myself, I forgive myself, I forgive myself, I forgive myself, I forgive myself, I forgive myself."

As you go through your day keep affirming and speaking the following words: "I am love. I am lovable. I love with an open heart. I love myself. I forgive myself. I forgive others. I am open to the compassion of Divine Source. I have healthy loving relationships. I love my body. I love my life."

Practical tools for everyday living can be found in 'The Processing Toolbox' on page 205.

Week Three: Day 19

Freedom & Communication

Today is Day 19 of your visits to your peace and gratitude garden. You have created such a peaceful center to visit, bringing your love and energy. Today you have brought with you another beautiful word of intention to seed in your garden, 'Freedom': free to be yourself. You deeply value freedom, an important segment of your creations here.

List five things for which you are really grateful in your life right now. Feel and connect to those feelings, and feel gratitude expanding throughout your body, giving you a great vibrational flow with which begin your morning.

1. I am responsible for my perceptions and feelings
2.
3.
4.
5.

Leaning into your tree, breathe and ground yourself into your body. Breathe into your fifth center, the throat chakra, which is sky-blue in color, located at the base of the throat. It controls the true meaning of communication, psychic consciousness, hearing, speaking and listening, listening to the wisdom of your soul. Breathe in and speak the following words: "I joyfully speak my truth. I express myself with clarity and courage. I joyfully share my creative gifts with the world. I communicate easily. I listen deeply to the wisdom of my soul. I am authentic."

Notice any negative feelings or beliefs that may come up as you speak these words.

You may notice that you are feeling like you are not able to express yourself well; you may feel afraid to speak up and speak your truth; you do not feel heard; you have the impression that nobody listens to you.

What does 'freedom' mean to you?

Do you believe that your body is communicating to you?

One of the first ways to claim back your power is through speech.

What keeps you going?

What does speaking your truth mean to you?

Are you standing in your truth, being courageous and expressing your feelings in a positive but firm way?

What negative feelings, beliefs, or stories—that no longer serve you—are you releasing today? Write a list of the negative feelings and do your daily ritual of burning the old suppressed feelings, habits, beliefs and thoughts that are not positive.

What are you claiming for yourself now?

As you go throughout your day, keep speaking the words: "I joyfully speak my truth. I express myself with clarity and courage. I joyfully share my creative gifts with the world. I communicate easily. I listen deeply to the wisdom of my soul. I am authentic. I am the seeker of my own truth."

Practical tools for everyday living can be found in 'The Processing Toolbox' on page 205.

Week Three: Day 20

Inner Vision

It is Day 20 of seeding your peace and gratitude garden. Are you loving your inner garden, which you have been cultivating with so much care, love, and joy? You have stayed committed these past 20 days, cultivating this relationship to peace that is so important to you. This is now your own inner sanctuary to which you can and must retreat any time throughout your day. It is your private paradise that you have created with your love, your passion, and your devotion to your life. You are living the dream: what is your dream? What is the big dream in your life?

List five things for which you are really grateful in your life right now. Feel the feelings of gratitude expand throughout your body, giving you a great vibrational flow with which to begin your morning.

1. I am dreaming the conscious dream
2.
3.
4.
5.

Breathe and ground yourself into your body. Placing your awareness in your sixth center, breathe into this third-eye chakra, deep indigo blue sky in color, located at the center of your forehead. Balanced, this chakra governs the imagination, and is also known as your vision center and your power of intuition center. The positive spin here will assist you in feeling peace and harmony, as you bring your vision and your true nature into resonance with your spirit.

Breathe in and speak the following words: "I SEE. I honor my crystal clear insight. I am open to the powerful magic of my imagination. I claim my intuitive knowing. I create beautiful dreams, beginning with my peace and gratitude garden. I am a visionary."

As you fly high above your life, look down and see what it looks like from above.

What is the big dream?

What is your vision of what you want to create?

Do you believe that you can manifest your dreams?

What is fulfilling?

How did you get here?

Do you trust what you see, and trust that still small voice from within?

Are you able to freely flow into the infinite potential of your imagination?

Notice any negative feelings or beliefs that may arise as you speak these words. You may not resonate with some of the spoken words—they may bring up emotions for you, letting you know what other things you deeply want to acknowledge in your life.

What more do you want to claim? Choose?

What negative feelings, beliefs, or stories—that no longer serve you—are you releasing today? Breathe in and allow yourself to feel for a moment (without judgment) any beliefs that may arise. Are you ready to release and let go of those that no longer serve you? Make your list of negative feelings you are releasing, letting go of all negative thoughts. Burn your list. You are choosing positive, loving thoughts only.

Breathe deeply and speak the following words, as you go throughout your day: "I choose to see. I honor my insight. I am open to the powerful magic of my imagination. I claim my intuitive knowing. I create beautiful dreams, beginning with my peace and gratitude garden. I am a visionary."

Practical tools for everyday living can be found in 'The Processing Toolbox' on page 205.

Week Three: Day 21

Higher Consciousness & Unity

It is Day 21 of creating your peace and gratitude garden. Your imagination is soaring with all kinds of new ideas and inspiration. You value your sense of peace and freedom, and you value the relationship you have with yourself and the Divine. You have cultivated your desire for solitude. On this very special day you have brought along another important stepping stone on which to paint your sacred word. Today's stone is 'Unity"—unity with your Divine Source.

List five things for which you are really grateful in your life right now. Allow the feelings of gratitude to expand throughout your body, giving you a great foundation on which to begin your morning. What is your dominant feeling of choice today?

1. I am grateful for all of my lessons
2.
3.
4.
5.

Hugging your tree, you are feeling eternally grateful. This daily grounding has really been helping you feel connected to the earth: helping you experience your own roots extending deep into the earth. As you breathe and ground yourself into your body, you breathe into your seventh chakra, located at the highest point of your body, the crown of your head. This chakra is connected to your pineal gland and its color is violet. It governs the consciousness of spiritual awakening, inner wisdom, and the gifts of enlightenment.

Breathe in and speak the following words: "I am united with all that is. I am grateful. I am deeply connected to Spirit. I am one with the Divine. Bliss awakens within my heart."

Notice any negative feelings or beliefs that may come up as you speak these words.

Notice any old feelings that make you feel afraid to express your authentic spiritual beliefs. Do you feel separate from your Divine Source? What about beliefs of feeling isolated or feeling alone?

What spiritual practices inspire you?

Have you experienced a lack of inspiration recently?

Do you pray and meditate?

Do you feel connected to Source?

Do you feel in unity and connected to all of life?

What are you claiming for yourself now?

What negative feelings, beliefs, or stories—that no longer serve you—are you releasing today? Breathe in and allow yourself to feel for a moment (without judgment) any beliefs that may arise. Are you ready to release and let go of those that no longer serve you? Make your list of negative feelings. You are releasing and letting go of all negative thoughts. Burn your list. You are choosing only positive, loving thoughts.

Breathe and speak the following words throughout your day: "I am united with all that is. I am grateful. I am peaceful. I am deeply connected to spirit. I am one with the Divine. Bliss awakens within my heart."

Practical tools for everyday living can be found in 'The Processing Toolbox' on page 205.

Dear Divine Being of Love,

Thank you for shining your light and for making a huge difference for us all. In the last 21 days, you have planted your garden with powerful seeds of love. You have carefully planted your precious stepping stones, leading you deeper into your inner sanctuary. The World thanks you and honors you for your contribution to Peace on Earth. Your heart is filled with gratitude and compassion for yourself and others. You are devoted to self-love, claiming your prosperity. You fully accept and trust the Divine in yourself. You celebrate your passion, enjoying life, expressing your joy and your truth. You honor your commitments, choosing your power in every conscious 'now' moment as you live your life in freedom, united with your Source, in Oneness with all.

Please revisit your inner sanctuary daily, watering the garden with your love.

~Kornelia

Practical Tools

⸏⊶⊙⊷⊙⊶⊙⊶⊶

A Toolbox For
Everyday Living

· Anger Management 101 | *page 209*
· Kornelia's Emotional Processing Technique | *page 219*
· The Art of Releasing Fear | *page 225*
· The Script by Karol Truman | *page 229*
· Short Three-Step Peace Process | *page 233*

This toolbox is created for you to use in the same way you would use a toolbox in your household if you had a kitchen plumbing issue. When you turn the water on you expect the water (emotion) to come out of the faucet and flow. When the flow is blocked, you get a toolbox to help you get the water flowing again. This is the metaphor I would like you to use for this toolbox. If your 'water' gets backed up as you are progressing through the peace practice, and if you are experiencing anger, then grab the appropriate 'tool' - 'Anger Management 101' - to help you express your anger in a healthy way.

When you are feeling hurt and in emotional pain, you want to begin an inner-dialog. Reach into the toolbox and select the tool 'Kornelia's Emotional Processing Technique'. That will help you to heal the wound.

When you feel a lot of fear, and you feel paralyzed, not being able to move forward, enter into an intimate relationship with fear, feeling it fully in the body as if it were really happening. To help with this, reach into the toolbox and retrieve the tool 'The Art of Releasing Fear.'

If you want to get to the DNA level of emotional wounding, 'The Script' by Karol Truman is a very helpful core tool.

May these tools on how to process, express, and transmute your human emotions be helpful on your path to peace.

May they be of service to you! May they help you to feel, process and release your old feelings, heal your emotional core wounds, and learn how to be liberated from your anger through your everyday life experiences.

May you experience, peace, harmony, and vitality in your physical body. Many blessings to you and your body.

> *"Is this pill really an effective pill? Is this process really an effective process?" Anything that causes you to allow what you desire is the process of coming into alignment. And so, we're not, in any way, validating or invalidating anything. Many offer their "dog and pony show" as being the one that works. And good for all of them. We applaud anything that assists someone in allowing the Well-being, that they so much want and deserve, to flow.*
>
> *~Abraham*

The key to peace is to release
the anger from within your
physical body & embrace
the freedom that is your truth.

Allow yourself to feel everything.
Feel it to the utmost
without covering it up.

Release the feeling. Let it go

Anger Management 101

The Physical Body

Everybody has anger, and everybody could use 'Anger Management 101'. All of us have our own truth to discover, and the best way to do that is to uncover the anger. If you are claiming any illness in your body, it is an opportunity to discover if and where you are suppressing any emotion (anger) in your body that wants to be acknowledged and released.

When I talk to people and clients about getting in touch with their anger, it amazes me how many say to me, "I am fine, I don't have any anger." Or, they say my talk about anger, or my book, would help a person whom they know. They bypass themselves completely. They don't get angry, but instead project the energy onto some other persons, wanting to fix them instead of getting in contact with their own anger.

The Bully

A perfect opportunity for the release of a feeling of powerlessness came when a man rented a room in my house. He passed all the background checks. He seemed very conscious, with a positive outlook about his life, and I felt really good about renting a room to him. After he moved in though, everything changed very fast and nothing he had said seemed to be true. My roommate and I were both feeling bullied by him, which brought up the feeling of not being safe in my own home. When I asked him to move out, he said I couldn't make him! This brought up a feeling of helplessness and powerlessness for me, and it made me very, very upset - actually enraged inside. Because I know how this process works, I trusted that after releasing the energy, I would be able to come back and approach him from an empowered place of not feeling victimized. I did the anger management process, the energy shifted, and shortly thereafter he moved out.

This type of bullying behavior can and does show up in the workplace, and it happens to both men and women. I know a man, who was working for a small business, whose boss was a very angry person who continuously projected his anger onto his employees. This type of working environment is very hostile, and yet the boss was always wondering why his turnover was so high, and why he could not retain his employees. Although the person on the receiving end of this bullying was also a man, he felt scared, stuck, and that his survival was at stake. I wonder how many people feel stuck in an environment where they don't feel supported? After many conversations about what he was feeling, followed by releasing those feelings, the employee claimed more of his power and made the choice to leave that environment. With the conscious awareness of this lesson, he is now free to create and attract a more loving environment that is more in alignment with his truth.

Anger Is The Catalyst

When we get angry or upset, the event, person, or situation that is triggering us is acting as a catalyst to release a feeling that is no longer serving us. This awareness requires courage, and it takes willingness to look and feel what this is about for us, release and let it go.

What pisses me off, what makes me angry has nothing to do with you, so don't take personally your being the catalyst activating my fire. Because of the experience, I can use that fire responsibly to create change. I accept and I know the anger is serving me to claim my power - not by force, but through conscious awareness.

Your Anger Is Your Gold

Love your anger/fire, be conscious of it and let burn away all that is not the truth within you. Your anger is your gold. It is never about the other person, it is your anger. When anger gets activated within you, it really is a blessing. It is an opportunity for the release of the energy which lay dormant within the body prior to the activation. It is an opportunity to discover what is underneath that anger, as well as an opportunity to love yourself through the fire.

When we get triggered, it is time to mirror and to hold space for each other. Becoming conscious of our feelings, we are able to transmute matter into mystical consciousness. "Thank you for mirroring my shadow so beautifully. It hurts so good." (Our shadow sides are 'not so acceptable' energies we don't want to see about ourselves, and our core fear in life mirrors them to us.)

Your Body - Your Best Friend

By bringing your conscious awareness to your body and using your body as a tool for transformation, you can remember and access your true essence. You gain physical, mental and emotional empowerment, plus radiant wellbeing, when you take responsibility and cultivate a harmonious relationship with your body. You are blessed with youthfulness and life. You have an open invitation, if you choose to use it, to become intimate with your body, curious about the dialog and messages that the body is ready to share with you - waiting for you to acknowledge its pure intelligence and wisdom. Your body is always in communication with you, so use it as your best friend who has your back, and you its. Become your body's cheerleader. As well as being the home housing your Spirit, it is your Spiritual Master, signaling you to engage in a sensational intimate relationship with it.

Remember, we have been unconscious and separate from the inherent intelligence in the body. Societal conditioning and programming has made us suppress and ignore our own issues, which is one reason why there is so much anger and depression. We have found many possible modes of band-aids in the form of addictions to cover up what our body is trying to communicate to us. The body knows that it is being ignored, and it is expressing symptoms to get your attention. The body is doing and behaving exactly as it was designed to do: to be of service to you. When we decide to honor the messages that our body has for us, then healing can take place on all levels.

To prevent the body from becoming ill (storing emotions), you need to be open and willing to feel all your feelings/emotions, rather than suppress or store them in the body. By being conscious and open to discovering whatever messages your body is trying to communicate to you, with the positive intent to decode the messages, the body will continuously mirror to you your thoughts and your emotions.

Our body remembers all of the past trauma, wounds, and pain it has ever experienced. It remembers everything. It is our job to take our power back by loving our body and consciously receiving the messages it is communicating to us. Our body is our dream machine, the vehicle which, in combination with our emotions and our mind, is helping us to make your dreams come true. The most important thing to remember is that we are here to feel good, and feeling good is the fastest way to manifest our desires. If we are suppressing issues, anger, emotions, or depression, this will keep us from creating a reality that is in alignment with our truth.

The Emotion of Anger

The emotion of anger is sometimes felt as resentment, sarcasm, frustration, argumentativeness, annoyance, aggressiveness, jealousy, or boiling feelings. It is really very simple when we look at all the reasons why we get angry. For men, this sometimes seems to be more challenging than for women. Men have always been taught to be strong, and they have not been encouraged to think or feel with their hearts, which, on some level, they have been made to believe is a weakness. When I ask men how they feel, I usually get an answer back from their left brain.

> We can hold space for each other to feel our feelings fully,
> to feel the anger, and let it move through.

Don't be afraid of your anger. It is energy in motion, it is not bad, it is not wrong. There is nothing wrong with you. Feel it. Feel it all fully. Allow the feelings to come up and give voice to your feelings, then release them and let them go. The anger will pass.

Anger Not Expressed

I am so over the being-nice part, or the cover-up part; that passive-aggressive behavior turned inward is so unattractive, unhealthy. It ages people. I am so over people projecting their anger onto others, as this, too, is such unattractive, bullying behavior. I am also over judgments slinging back and forth, behavior likened to a bunch of 3-year olds who don't know any better. Yet - this has been our conditioning and our training. This is what we were taught to do.

I am so over the part that says to hide it from the children, when the truth is that they are wired for a new way. They are our bridge. They provide our triggers, they can be our space holders. Children do not have all that suppression that you are carrying. They don't have an 'onion' with layers of anger to peel. If the kids today can give blow jobs at the age of 10, they can hold space for us, after we have had our meltdowns. This could be the flip-side.

Anger turned inward and suppressed will turn into resentment, depression, sabotage, quick temper, lashing out at people, loneliness, isolation, fear, tightness, paralyzation, powerlessness, weakness in the body, shallow breathing, and feelings of lack, limitation, victimization.

Depression

The best thing to do for people who are depressed -be it friends, family members, neighbors, or colleagues - is to reach out to them and get them really, really pissed off. When people are depressed, they have given up. They are too paralyzed to move forward. They are feeling lost and defeated. If you know someone who is depressed, go to them; offer them the space, offer them your hand, and give them the opportunity to be heard and witnessed. Give them the opportunity to get good and pissed off, to bring that energy from depression up into anger. Ask them what it is they are so depressed about, ask them what they are feeling, and let the anger burn that depression away. Sometimes we need someone to hold our hand until we can hold it for ourselves. Depression is the one of the lowest of feelings, and people who are depressed could use a hand, and someone to hold space for them. I have seen this work time and time again with clients and friends, including myself. When I feel powerless or feel depressed, it is time to get pissed and get that energy moving. By feeling our feelings and giving voice to our feelings, the need to judge anything falls away, just like the feelings do. Everything wants to be loved, and everything wants to be acknowledged.

Using Anger As A Tool

Using anger positively as a tool will give you energy, creative purpose, freedom, liberation, space, connection, unity, strength, abundance, health, harmony and well-being in the body - and is the best anti-aging cream on the market. Why? Because as you are moving the energy, now new light can move into those cells. No longer holding on tight, there is a relaxed feeling, a receptive feeling. Be the compassionate witness for yourself and others. Bring your awareness to the suffering you are experiencing and allow yourself to be present to your pain, anger, and suffering, without shying away. Let your life be opened by this experience, without resistance.

Step One:

An event happens and you get triggered. This could be in the work-place, in your relationships, or in your environment. Whatever an-gers you is never ever about a person, situation or event. Bring the energy back to yourself and how you feel by being triggered. Then start the dialog with, "I feel.... I feel angry right now. I feel upset. I feel...." Go deeper and bring the feeling up to the surface: " I feel like I don't matter. I feel like I am small. I feel like I am worthless. I feel lied to. I feel cheated. I feel betrayed. I feel I can't trust anymore. I feel powerless. I feel like I have tried everything and nothing works. I feel ashamed. I feel not good enough. I feel afraid to communicate. I feel it in my throat. I feel it in the pit of my stomach. I feel it in my heart. I don't feel loved. I don't feel valued. I don't feel appreciated. I don't feel heard. I don't feel honored. I don't feel safe. I feel disre-spected."
Those are old feelings that you are releasing now.

Unhealthy '1970's style' ways to express your fire
- *Suppressing the energy in the body*
- *Projecting onto the other person or event*
- *Acting like nothing is wrong*
- *Taking drugs, or drinking your worries down*
- *Unconsciously complaining, or taking the victim role (they did this*
  to me, poor me)
- *'Going postal', hitting, or harming another*
- *Shooting back verbally at, or taking revenge on the person who triggered you*

Healthy ways to express your anger (fire):
- *Go into your 'anger management room' and let it out*
- *Accept responsibility for your thoughts, actions, and feelings*
- *Take ownership of your own anger*
- *"I accept. I choose to release. I feel mad as hell."*
- *What are you feeling angry about?*
- *"I am choosing to let it all go"*

· *Scream out at the top of your lungs, or scream your head off!*
· *From the core of your solar plexus in the middle of your stomach,*
  feel everything
· *Howl like a bitch in heat*
· *Cry, cry, cry - weep uncontrollably*
· *Use the F-word as many times you possibly can: "I'm so f... pissed off, are you kidding me..."*
· *Stomp up and down, or do a dance*
· *Call a friend, ask for this friend to witness and hold the space*
· *Do whatever you can do to get the fire out*

**In any situation in which you are claiming your power
ask yourself the following question:
"What is the most powerful choice I can make right now?"**

Step Two:

Nothing ever goes away until we feel all that is there to be felt and released. After you have had the opportunity to let your anger/emotion out, give yourself some space to really understand what the experience was about for you. What was the lesson, and what approach would you like to take now that you have released this energy?

Have compassion for yourself when triggered, because it hurts and is painful. The people/situations that are triggering you are gifting you. Thank them for triggering you and for mirroring your shadow back to you - even if you have to thank them silently. It is a wonderful gift. Offering them gratitude, compassion, and most of all consciousness, is the key to your liberation. Offering radical forgiveness to yourself and the person who hurt you is your choice. Thank them for helping YOU. The key is awareness and applying these tools after having released your anger.

It is through these experiences that you have released powerlessness. Congratulations! What a victory for you, and what a gift. Now replace the feeling of powerlessness - and to ground in a new and empowered way of being for yourself, here are some beautiful mantras. Speak these powerful mantras into being: "I choose and claim my power here. I feel so very powerful. I am an empowered being. I choose to forgive. I choose love. I embrace unconditionally all of myself. I choose my power. I claim my life. I choose to be at peace."

Peace begins within You, yourself; take radical responsibility for being the peacemaker. Learning to release your fire - your anger - is one of the most loving peaceful acts you can offer this planet. War is the extreme action of angry people, and even though we have war going on in different parts of the world, or right here at home, the most powerful thing you can do is take care of yourself, bring yourself into harmony and peace and be that role model for others.

Become a space holder for yourself,
holding space for others in the workplace
and in your relationships.

Be the peace you wish to see.

Kornelia's Emotional Processing Technique

You can do this processing inquiry with anything that is causing you to experience emotional or mental discomfort. This process gets you out of your head and establishes a dialog with yourself. It moves you into communication with yourself.

"Processing is a form of self-inquiry—a way of looking at our egoic self. "Ego" refers to the personality structure, which results from childhood and worldly conditioning. The term "to process" means to examine and to inquire deeply into the nature of our conditioned and unbalanced egoic programming with the intention of moving our awareness into balance and truth. We process our consciousness in order to become clear and ultimately to find our wholeness."
~Leslie Temple-Thurston

There are really only a handful of core emotional wounds that are attached to beliefs we have about ourselves. Do you keep repeating the same patterns and are you having the same experiences over and over again? It's critical that we are in emotional balance when we are creating. Our Beliefs and Emotionshave to be congruent with each other in order to manifest what we desire.

You might identify with one or more of these feelings:
- Abandonment
- Betrayal
- Unworthy/not good enough
- Shame (the ugliest one) We have been conditioned to feel shameful all our life.Think about how many times you have been told as a child, or an adult, to be ashamed of yourself.
- Survival needs

· Victim/Savior
· Separation from God/Source

To best clear these core wounds, they have to be felt and cleared out of the emotional body. These wounds can be very painful to feel, but it will pass. Releasing this old energy and moving it out of our body will allow more health and vitality to enter its space. Remember, the lower and higher energies can not exist in the same space; releasing the lower energies makes room for new energies to come in. This will allow you to feel lighter and happier.

This is a missing piece that the movie 'The Secret' didn't tell us - or 'The Law of Attraction' hype left out a few years back. We can sit and think positively all day long doing affirmations or intending positive thoughts, but if we have lower emotional wounds and hidden beliefs attached to them, all the envisioning won't help. You cannot talk yourself out of feeling pain or grief. There is no shortcut and no getting around it. This pressure from your emotional wounds can be felt in the body and has to be released. This pressure can also cause illness and disease.

Most of the time when we get triggered (having our buttons pushed) it is by someone with whom we have a close relationship. When an event happens and you get triggered emotionally, notice first where you feel the emotion in your body!

Ask yourself these questions:
Why am I angry, pissed off or hurt?

What is this about for me?

Write down: "I feel angry, sad, fearful, ashamed, guilt, enraged, hope-less, helpless, powerless, jealous, resentment, or paralyzed because..."

Below are some questions to consider when we get triggered. Use the questions to practice this technique.

What is this about for me?

Who is the person or situation that is causing me to feel so up-set?

How does this situation make me feel? (Don't hold back; be picky.)

Where do I feel this in my body?

What is this situation/person doing to/for me?

Now go deeper; what else does this emotion bring up for you?

Go into the storyline of what happened and name the word on the list that you can identify with:

I feel..... abandoned..... betrayed..... worthless..... not good enough..... shame.....

You have found the word on the list; for example: "I feel abandoned by Oscar; every time he tells me he is going to change, he does not. He keeps telling me that he will come home shortly - and does not show up for days. This makes me feel abandoned by him and makes me feel like he does not care about me. The other part that really upsets me is that I keep taking him back every time, over and over and over again."

Why do I do this to myself? What part of myself am I abandoning?

What story would I have to believe to be true to myself?

You found the core wound of abandonment here. This is your opportunity to really go deep into the feeling of abandonment and feel where else in your life have you felt this before. Track it back; *do you feel have other people abandoned you? Are you ready to release and heal this pattern?*

Did you feel like you were abandoned by your family? Your Mom, Dad, or both?

The key here is to fully feel this emotion and welcome it in. Cry, sob, scream, call or talk to someone you trust, someone who can listen to you without trying to fix anything or make you better. Ask them to witness you in the pain that you are feeling; you just want someone to listen to you. Don't make the feeling go away and don't try to push it away; we have always pushed our feelings away. Stay with it. Feeling it is Healing it. Acknowledge how much pain you are in and have compassion for yourself.

Soon you will start to feel better because once and for all you have given space and love for this emotion to be felt - instead of its being covered up, hidden, or denied. You are claiming this aspect of yourself back into wholeness. The next Oscar won't need to play that role for you because you cleared it. Now you can feel appreciation for Oscar for his having triggered you, and for his playing that role for you so you can clear your feeling of abandonment.

Please write this down:
> *"I allow myself to feel this emotion once and for all. I know this will pass. I am loving this part of myself."*

Was abandonment one of your core beliefs?
> *"I release it now with my conscious intent, I am releasing the core wound of abandonment. The truth is, I am not abandoned; I am right here and I am safe. I am releasing the emotion of abandonment; I am transmuting this energy into love, infusing it with unconditional love."*

My new belief is:
> *"I am safe and secure within myself. I allow myself this space."*

Please note that at the time of processing, when you have just released the emotion, you are not yet at a place to make yourself feel safe.

After 24 hours, check in again and you will see that you feel lighter and better, and can now close out this wound/experience with your new belief.

Your new belief is:

"I am safe and secure, I feel safe and secure within Me, I feel safe and I trust Me. I will not abandon Me. I love Me."

Did you have a belief of not feeling worthy?

"I release this unworthiness now with my conscious intent. I am releasing this core wound of not feeling worthy or good enough. The truth is I am worthy and I am good enough. I am releasing this feeling and emotion. I am transmuting this energy into love, infusing myself with unconditional love. My new belief is: I am worthy of love and abundance. I am willing to embrace my worthiness. It is my divine birthright to feel worthy."

After 24 hours come back and close out this wound, knowing you have just cleared the core wound of worthlessness out of your energy field.

Your new belief is:

"I am worthy, I feel worthy, I feel worthy in my energy expression, I express my worthiness through my physical body, I see my worthiness reflected back to me in all my relationships."

Kornelia@KorneliaStephanie.com
Inspire · Empower · Connect
www.KorneliaStephanie.com

The Art of Releasing Fear From Your Life

A 30-Day Challenge

Get intimate with your fear and feel it fully. Release it from your physical body once and for all. Everything wants to be loved and accepted. Everything wants to be felt, and everything needs to be felt—even your fears. All you need to do is go in and feel the fear as if it were happening right now. Then, as if by magic, it is gone. Nothing has any power over you, only that to which you give your power.

You have to be willing to get intimate with your fears all the way. It takes a lot of courage and consciousness, however—and it is a very liberating process.

FEAR: False Evidence Appearing Real

Most of our fear is not real; it is in our head. It only feels real because we are energetically paralyzed by it. We allow it to stop us from taking action. What is happening in our minds seems absolutely real, and we can't move one way or the other because fear has us in its grip.

Say: *"I am afraid"; or "I feel scared"; or "I am in fear."*

Mostly fear is kept at arm's length, just outside of ourselves—instead of being invited in. In a way, the fear is victimizing us.

Do you hear yourself telling the same fear story, over and over again?

YOU can pretend that fear is knocking on the door, it is wanting to come into your house, you answer the door. All you want to do is run, or slam the door shut. Instead, answer the door and say, "I am ready to invite you in. Even though I feel afraid of you, I am inviting you into my home. I don't want to be afraid anymore. I don't want to fear you anymore. I want to love you free." Invite the fear in.

The antidote to fear is to welcome it into your physical body.

To release fear from your life, you have to be willing to do the dance, to be courageous and process everything that presents itself to you as fear. Feel it, bring it into your experience, get it out of your head, feel it fully as if it were happening momentarily. Then, watch it melt away like magic.

Are you ready for your 30-day challenge?

The Practice

Write the day and date on a sticky note, and make a list of all the fears you have right now.

Example: Saturday, November 5, 2015

Fears
- not moving forward
- running out of money, not able to pay my bills
- not getting any work
- not getting any clients
- not successful at setting up my new business
- not being accepted
- being antisocial
- not finding my purpose
- not taking actions toward my dreams
- public speaking
- shining my own light
- being powerful

- · not getting a job
- · fear of success
- · fear of failure
- · fear of not being good enough

Next, sit in a quiet place with your sticky note. How does it feel not to be moving forward, stuck, like you are failing and not succeeding? Just sit still and feel it. Feel it fully, allowing your whole body any sensations that arise. Now imagine the world is watching you, YOU, not being able to move forward. Everybody sees how stuck you are. You have just expanded yourself out into the world and are living your fear as if it were real, allowing yourself to be witnessed by an audience. How does that feel? You have always carried that fear in your head, believing it, and now you have made it physical by feeling it fully, as if it were real. *Now release all these feelings. Let them go.*

Feel into the next fear on your note (running out of money, not being able to pay your bills.) How does it feel to not have any money; to not be able to pay your bills? Really feel it fully—feel it all. Feel the fear of all of it—fully. Now, imagine the whole world knows that you ran out of money and can't pay your bills. Does that make you feel embarrassed? What other feelings does that bring up in you? You have just expanded it out and now let it go. The key here is to feel all of this as if it were real, even though you know it is not.

The great thing is, you will notice in the coming days that this no longer has a pull on you; the feelings are no longer present. Remember, letting go of your fears is like peeling an onion, and if you have some deep ingrained fears, this layer may come back in about three months, another layer ready to be processed. And—now you know how to do it, and guess what? YOU are free. It is easy, though scary, to feel your fears. It is quite simple.

For fun, you could keep your stickies in a drawer and over time let go of more and more fears.

Feel the celebration of that—write it down—it will help you see how far you have come and what an amazing 'fear-buster' you are.

The wonderful thing is, by inviting your fears into your life, you make room for so much more bliss than you can possibly imagine.

Have fun facing your fears and be brave - you've got it.

2009 Script by Karol Truman

T he Author of the book Feelings Buried Alive Never Die, Karol was so generous to send me the script (below) to share with you in my book so that it may be of service to you all.

Using this script process any unresolved issues you have with anyone who stands out in your mind. Karol writes in her book that by "using this script feelings of resentment, hostility, animosity, anger, bitterness, or pride are often the culprits that stifle, suffocate, smother, choke, restrain or limit you. By using this script, you will resolve any deeply buried feelings entrenched inside of yourself. She also notes that you may use any higher power of your choice."

2009 Script

In the name of Spirit, Superconscious, Subconscious, Conscious, Higher Self, Heart, Mind, Will, Nervous System-Brain, Original Intelligence, RNA, DNA, and every genetic anomaly out of alignment with my pattern of perfection, please locate the origin of my Conscious and Subconscious destructive cellular memories which caused the incorrect perceptions that created feelings/thoughts/beliefs of _____.

Take each and every level, layer, area, and aspect of my Being to these origins. Analyze and resolve them perfectly with God the Father's truth.

Come forward through all generations of time and eternity, healing every event and its appendages based on the origins. Please do it according to God the Father's will, until I'm at the present — filled with light and truth, God's Immanence, peace and love, benevolence, forgiveness of myself for my imperfect perceptions, having compassion for every person, place, circumstance and event which contributed to any of these destructive cellular memories, feelings, thoughts, or beliefs.

With total forgiveness and unconditional love, I ask that my physical, mental, emotional, and spiritual memory of perfection resonate throughout my Being.

I choose Being (insert positive feeling/s):

I feel (same truth):

I AM (same truth):

(Replace previous feelings/thoughts/beliefs with the same desired truth on each line.)

It is done! It is healed! It is accomplished now!
Thank you all for coming to my aid and working together to help me rid my Being of stress, and attain the full measure of my creation. Thank you, thank you, thank you! I love you and praise God the Father from whom all blessings flow.

Now, all facets of my Being, please put this Scripting on automatic so it repeats itself throughout each and every cell and fiber of my Being every half hour of every day for the next 180 days (or however long is best for me), thereby re-storing perfectly healthy frequencies throughout my Being and returning me to my original purpose, power and magnificence!

And it is done!

Short Three-Step Peace Process

This short three-step process was founded by Sarah Hartzell.

Picture a time in your life when you were at peace with the world and also with yourself. Where were you, what did it feel like, what sensations did you have? Bring that vibration into your whole being now.
Say: *"I feel peaceful when......"*

What current situation or relationship is challenging you? What is it that needs to be acknowledged here?
Say: *"Peace for me in this situation would be......."*

Pledge one decisive action for the coming week in relation to the challenge.
Say: *"In the name of peace, I will........"*

Part Three

The New Spiritual Human: Change The World

"Our deepest fear is not that we are inadequate. Our deepest fear is that we are power-ful beyond measure. It is our light, not our darkness that most frightens us.

We ask ourselves, "Who am I to be brilliant, gor-geous, talented, fabulous?"

Actually, who are you not to be?

You are a child of God.

Your playing small does not serve the world.

There is nothing enlightened about shrinking so that other people won't feel insecure around you.

We are all meant to shine, as children do.

We were born to make manifest the glory of God that is within us.

It's not just in some of us; it is in everyone.

And as we let our light shine, we unconsciously give other people permission to do the same.

As we are liberated from our own fear, our presence automatically liberates others."

- Marianne Williamson

Holistic Reference Recommendations

Books For Your Medicine Cabinet
- *Peace: The Flip Side to Anger* by Kornelia Stephanie
- *You Can Heal Your Life* by Louise Hay
- *Feelings Buried Alive Never Die* by Karol Truman

Essential Books of the New Earth
- *The Power of Now* by Eckhart Tolle
- *A Return to Love* by Marianne Williamson
- *Loving What Is* by Byron Katie
- *The Passion Test* by Janet Bray Attwood and Chris Attwood
- *Ask and it Shall be Given* by Esther and Jerry Hicks

Articles
- 'Drugged Into Oblivion: Nearly 60 Percent Of All U.S. Adults Are On Prescription Drugs' by Michael Snyder
- 'With Newest Arrest, The NFL Should Impose A Unique Mandatory Anger Management Program' by Roger Groves

Body, Mind, and Spirit

For a peaceful, holistic healing environment, practice yoga for life. There are many yoga teachers to help support you in achieving overall health and well-being. Find a yoga studio near you and make yoga your partner in achieving health and wellness. If you are a just beginning yoga, I recommend Hatha Yoga, which focuses on basic postures. Also, there is a great online yoga program at Gaiam Yoga.com or yogajournal.com.

Sound Healing
· Marianne Green, Transformation through Sacred Sounds
"Sound Vibrations Unlock the Gates to our Inner Temple.
Healing takes place when Body, Emotions, Mind and Spirit
are working together as ONE."
http://www.sphericalimprovisations.com

· Kevin Doheny
"Sound freeing your thoughts to raise the consciousness
of a world"
http://www.soundmindbodyhealing.com/index.html

· Tina Turner
Sarvesham Svastir Bhavatu (Peace Mantra)
https://www.youtube.com/watch?v=6XP-f7wPM0A

· Tom Kenyon
Song of the New Earth
http://tomkenyon.com

Marketing & Creative Master
· Nisha Bhatt
Creating inspiring marketing, graphics, illustrations, and
websites that reflect you through conscious, creative solutions
http://www.nishabhatt.com

Universal Wholeness Coaches
(certified through Kornelia's coaching program)

· Robyn Pipkin
Empowerment through Yoga and Empowerment Coaching
http://www.yournexthighestexpression.com

· Charleen Hess
Hair Stylist/Educator | Wholeness Life Coach | Personal Trainer
http://www.charleenhess.com

Law of Attraction Coach

· Wendy Binggeli
"The Art of Manifesting More in your Life"
http://www.loacoach.ca

· Kornelia Stephanie
"Living your life as a powerful co-creator on purpose in 100 alignment with you."
http://www.korneliaStephanie.com

Video

· Anthony Robbins coaches little girl who wanted to commit Suicide 'Hanna's Story'
http://training.rmtcenter.com/hannahsstory1?imt=1&utm_campaign=Hannah&utm_source=FB&utm_medium=PPC&utm_content=Hannah+-LA

Drugged Into Oblivion: Nearly 60 Percent Of All U.S. Adults Are On Prescription Drugs

Submitted by IWB, on November 4th, 2015 By Michael Snyder

If you have a health problem, even if it is just an imaginary one, some giant pharmaceutical company out there is probably making a pill for it. According to shocking new research published in the Journal of the American Medical Association, 59 percent of all U.S. adults are on at least one prescription drug, and 15 percent of all U.S. adults are on at least five prescription drugs. These numbers have never been higher, and they tell us that the United States is the most drugged nation on the entire planet. And it turns out that pushing these drugs on the American people is extremely profitable. For instance, Americans spent 100 billion dollars on cancer drugs alone last year. That isn't "million" with an "m" – that is "billion" with a "b". The profits that some of these pharmaceutical companies are making are absolutely obscene, and it is our pain and suffering that is making them rich.

So why is prescription drug use rising so rapidly? As noted above, 15 percent of us are now taking 5 or more of these drugs on a regular basis, but back in 1999 that number was sitting at just 8.2 percent. This newly released report blames much of the problem on obesity... The population is getting older, but that doesn't explain it, Kantor said. The pattern looks more related to obesity, which is steadily rising, More than two-thirds of the adult U.S. population is overweight or obese, and many suffer the heart disease, diabetes and other metabolic disorders that go along with being too heavy. And without a doubt, we have an epidemic of obesity in the United States. The following facts on American obesity come from from my recent article entitled "America #1? 36 Facts That Prove That The United States Is An 'Exceptional' Nation"...

#1 According to a brand new report that was just released by the Organization for Economic Cooperation and Development, the United States has the fattest population in the entire industrialized world by a wide margin.

#2 That same report from the OECD also found that we are number one in child obesity. In fact, at 38 percent our rate of childhood obesity is even higher than our overall rate of obesity.

#3 According to USA Today, the obesity rate in the United States has more than doubled over the past 25 years.

But the truth is that obesity is only part of the story. Drug use of all types is soaring, and commercials for the latest and greatest drugs seem to run around the clock on virtually every television network. Here are some more specific numbers from this newly released report...

· In the study, blood pressure drugs were among the most prescribed, increasing from 20% of adults in 1999-2000 to 27% in 2011-2012.

· Statins increased from 6.9% to 17%; antidepressants increased from 6.8% 13%; antidiabetic drugs increased from 4.6% to 8.2%;and tranquilizers and sedatives increased from 4.2% to 6.1%.

The increase in the use of antidepressants really disturbs me. They are often prescribed needlessly, and they can have some extremely negative side effects.

In particular, I think that it is important to mention that nearly every single mass shooter in the United States in recent years has been on antidepressants. The mainstream media never talks about this connection because the pharmaceutical companies purchase gobs of advertising time from them. But the reality of the matter is that these drugs can cause people to behave in extremely irrational ways. Even the Mayo Clinic admits this...

Most antidepressants are generally safe, but the Food and Drug Administration requires that all antidepressants carry black box warnings, the strictest warnings for prescriptions.In some cases, children, teenagers and young adults under 25 may have an increase in suicidal thoughts or behavior when taking antidepressants, especially in the first few weeks after starting or when the dose is changed.

Of course that is a very watered down version of the truth, and if you start seriously digging into this you will soon discover a whole host of absolutely horrifying stories.

But the pharmaceutical companies are never going to stop what they are doing, because it is making them exceedingly wealthy. As I mentioned above, Americans spent 100 billion dollars on cancer drugs last year, and the big drug firms love milking cancer patients for all that they are worth. According to NBC News, two of the latest cancer drugs that have been developed "are priced at $12,500 a month".

How do executives at those companies sleep at night?

They are getting rich from price gouging cancer patients.

How disgraceful is that?

Here are some more statistics about the drugging of America that come fromone of my previous articles...
　· According to the CDC, approximately 9 out of every 10 Americans that are at least 60 years old say that they have taken at least one prescription drug within the last month.
　· There is an unintentional drug overdose death in the United States every 19 minutes.
　· In the United States today, prescription painkillers kill more Americans than heroin and cocaine combined.
　· According to the CDC, approximately three quarters of a million people a year are rushed to emergency rooms in the United States because of adverse reactions to pharmaceutical drugs.
　The percentage of women taking antidepressants in America is

higher than in any other country in the world.

· Children in the United States are three times more likely to be prescribed antidepressants as children in Europe are.

· A shocking Government Accountability Office report discovered thatapproximately one-third of all foster children in the United States are on at least one psychiatric drug.

· A survey conducted for the National Institute on Drug Abuse found that more than 15 percent of all U.S. high school seniors abuse prescription drugs.

· Many of these antidepressants contain warnings that "suicidal thoughts" are one of the side effects that should be expected. The suicide rate for Americans between the ages of 35 and 64 rose by close to 30 percent between 1999 and 2010. The number of Americans that are killed by suicide now exceeds the number of Americans that die as a result of car accidents every year.

So what is your take on all of this?

Do you have any prescription drug horror stories to share?

Please feel free to participate in the discussion by posting a comment below...

http://investmentwatchblog.com/drugged-into-oblivion-nearly-60-percent-of-all-u-s-adults-are-on-prescription-drugs/

About the author: Michael T. Snyder is a graduate of the University of Florida law school and he worked as an attorney in the heart of Washington D.C. for a number of years. Today, Michael is best known for his work as the publisher of The Economic Collapse Blog (http://theeconomiccollapseblog.com/). Michael and his wife, Meranda, believe that a great awakening is coming and they are working hard to help bring renewal to America.

With Newest Arrest, The NFL Should Impose A Unique Mandatory Anger Management Program

September 18th, 2014 By Roger Groves

The NFL has the most highly skilled workforce of angry men on the planet apart from the military. They've been trained to be violent gladiators since prepubescence. Some had nurturing balanced households with highly disciplined fathers and mothers that trained them to leave the violence on the field. Some did not. Nowhere in the NFL training manual is there an exercise regimen that treats for the difference. Of the $9 billion of revenue shared between the NFL owners and the players, only a miniscule fraction is devoted to managing the players' violent side off the field.

Understandably, no business wants to drive up costs unnecessarily. But when you now have six headline-grabbing incidents within a few weeks, the most recent of which is Arizona Cardinals running back Jonathan Dwyer taken away in handcuffs from the practice field as later viewed by millions of fans, and when those incidents are more discussed than the game itself, the NFL has a necessary cost to bring about a change.

More graphic but still underreported are the finding of investigate reporters that at least 20 current players have been charged or convicted with assault or crimes of violence against those without uniforms. Of course the percentage of the total is small. There are 1,700 players in the NFL workforce on average each year. But the coveted NFL brand can be disproportionately damaged by that very small percentage of the total.

Is the NFL and each club going to play Russian Roulette, waiting to see which team gets shot with a new public relations nightmare? More importantly, do they wait for the guilt of wondering if they could have done more to counsel the people they picked as employees? Do they take their turn at yet another apology to more victims, families and fans? Or is there something else they can do more proactively that is more curative than reactive?

Since the NFL to date is always the last to know, and cannot seem to identify the at-risk players and provide assistance in advance, they should do what most corporations do when workforce behaviors need to be uniform – provide mandatory training to everyone in the workforce.

Anger is the root cause and common element of all these crimes against humanity, be it against a woman or a child. Controlling the anger is the goal. So why not take some of the billions of dollars and customize a program designed for these workers who are uniquely trained to be violent. That way, the NFL can better identify those who are at risk in advance and get the player help before the incident.

The NFL, for instance, could hire experts to develop assessment tools. All 32 clubs should be required to use them. The assessments should create a physiological profile with depth in the childhood history and family behavioral legacies. The assessments can take advantage of the substantial body of research, role playing and simulated exercises in the field of anger management. There are now avatars available to put the player in virtual reality schemes. They can be designed to place him in on-field, and off-field situations most ripe of angry encounters. Assessing the reactions, heart rate differences, and other medically and physiologically discernable differences are all state of the art methods. These methods are increasingly used for detecting and improving behaviors, including but not limited to implicit biases. Why not customize those evolving techniques for football biases and dispositions?

That is a better remedy than the current system. Clearly the NFL does not have a process that identifies and treats before the incidents occur. In each case they have been surprised and unable to quickly and correctly respond. Just as clearly, the NFL focus on punishing each player after the fact is not a good player management strategy. The problem of uniformity of treatment and finding the correct amount of punishment to fit the offense is the wrong business for the NFL and its team owners. They cannot win that game. But they can win the respect of players and fans if they become a leader in the caring field, caring enough to make treating others well a priority. The best way to do that is to work harder at creating a guidance system than on new uniform designs, spending more money on assessments that helps players before a crime occurs, than on punishing them once it happens.

Roger Groves is a Professor of Law and Director of the Business Law Program at Florida Coastal School of Law. Follow Roger on Twitter @rgroveslaw.

Together we are changing the world

My Mission

Empowering all into their authentic expression and sovereignty. Inspiring self-healing, self-love, self-leadership, self-empowerment. Returning to the basics of co-creating the New Earth, as embodied Divine Beings.

Together WE are Co-Creating our New Earth.

Now you are well on your way to really being able to feel all of yourself, to really being fully in your body. What a gift it is to be alive in a physical body. You came here to feel alive; allow yourself to feel the fullness of you.

Are you making daily choices that reflect the consciousness of unconditional love in the New Earth. Or, are you making daily choices that are still related to the Old Earth, exemplified by limitations, doubt, and mistrust?

In building a solid foundation for the New Earth, we as New Humans progress by embodying the knowing that we glean through our physical experiences and the choices we make. Our conscious focus and our daily choices are made based on unconditional love and compassion, trusting that the greater good for all is our pathway to JOY.

The What Is™ Game
Speak your world into being

I've created something very exciting to share with you that will support you even further in your evolution and expansion into your own greatness.

I am inviting you to come and play with me. It's time to have some fun.

I created a new game, The What Is™ Game, to inspire and empower us, to guide us into our own knowing and personal leadership. The world needs more of us who are ready to look inside ourselves, be our own gurus, our own leaders. We all have everything we need right inside ourselves, we just forget to look: there is no need to search outside of ourselves for answers, approval, and love, as so, so many do.

An example of the What Is™ Game

What is the word 'abundance'? The meaning can only be experienced by you, the person who is having the experience. Through the process of exploring your relationship to this word, it becomes a knowing, it becomes your truth, it becomes you. Otherwise it is just an idea from the collective, or from someone who is an expert on this word, this concept. Through the What Is™ Game, you now become your own expert on the meaning of this word.

Let's go back to the game word 'abundance.' If you are experiencing anything less than abundance in your physical reality contrast to what you are desiring, in other words—then this game is giving you the opportunity to release anything less than abundance out of your perception and reality.

Becoming an expert of the 'word' through your experience

Playing this game is your invitation to experience and embody the word, experience and live the word, know intimately the meaning behind the word. Confident in your knowing, you can be your own guru.

> "Self-confidence is the most basic and useful kind of faith. When you lack that kind of confidence or faith, you're likely to project it onto some external authority or object. That will, in turn, further weaken your self-confidence. So, if you want to strengthen your confidence or faith, withdraw your worship of external Gods and focus on your true inner nature." ~Karmapa

I have created an online structure and am inviting others to have fun co-creating with me, embodying and living the word in authentic, loving leadership, inspiring and touching heart-based living and thriving communities...for the greater good of ALL.

Want to come and join in? Receive daily inspirations? We are changing the game and making a difference—on purpose. The game provides ongoing support and fun for you, so read on...

How will playing the What Is™ Game help my life?

Playing this game will help you embody the power behind the words. Become an expert. It is not meant to complicate your life, rather, it has been created and designed to compliment your life.

JOY is the foundation for our New Earth.

The What Is™ Game is a spiritual, inspirational, fun, empowering, word and physical body game.

The New Spiritual-Human Love Protocol
—From Super Soldiers to Super Love Avatars

- The New Spiritual Human is willing to release all negative thoughts and feelings
- The New Spiritual Human knows to use anger as a tool to liberate oneself
- The New Spiritual Human practices the art of letting go for the utmost ease
- The New Spiritual Human reprograms oneself everyday with positivity
- The New Spiritual Human refuses to judge anyone, they look in the mirror first.
- The New Spiritual Human is deeply devoted to practice self love, emitting that frequency to all life.
- The New Spiritual Human loves the wounded child and the wounded ego with love, compassion, and understanding
- The New Spiritual Human chooses to retire the victim and the addict with love, compassion, and gratitude
- The New Spiritual Human embraces the innate ability to heal oneself.
- The New Spiritual Human knows to process fears into love
- The New Spiritual Human has the courage to take full responsibility and ownership for everything
- The New Spiritual Human chooses to re-claim our sovereign self empowerment
- The New Spiritual Human connects with nature, angels and source daily
- The New Spiritual Human sees the gift they are, sees the gift life is
- The New Spiritual Human shines BRIGHT, spreads love to all
- The New Spiritual Human shares joy for the greater good of all
- The New Spiritual Human leads by example and creates the world we want to live in.

Speak Your World Into Being

Daily inspirational messages and activations are posted five days a week. A message is waiting for you every morning when you get up: a living play-shop right at your fingertips. Every day you will get your spiritual workout. Activations, aligning with the New Earth consciousness, will help you let go of 'Old Earth' thought, emotions, feelings, beliefs, and energy that no longer serve you.

How will playing this game bring out your inner radiance? There is nothing more attractive than people who are confident in their knowing. Your daily personal engagement with this game will help you regain your inherent sense-of-self, your confidence!

Together we are changing the world, and this requires your input, your knowing, and your voice. I want you to bring your powerful energy and blessings to this experience. I want you to access the teacher within you that is all-knowing. I want you to activate your inner-student and add your voice, your personal contribution. Through this inner game, YOUR outer game becomes one of abundant JOY: for yourself, your family, and the world. Playing the game—embodying the word—consciously puts you in charge of your life: YOU—the radiant one who knows the power of the spoken word. YOU speak your new world into being.

We practice together in the online forum where we can share our experiences.
Every week there is a theme. Everybody benefits from the theme—individually and collectively.

How you play this game will change the world.

This experience is meant to change you forever. This is what life is about: to live, have our experiences, and then add our knowing into it. You will continually be releasing and letting go of thoughts, emotions, and beliefs that no longer serve your highest being.

Everything in your life that does not represent
the word that you are practicing
will be transmuted into JOY

Please visit my website: http://www.korneliaStephanie.com/members/
If you send an email to iampeace@korneliaStephanie.com you will receive a link to a free seven-day experience.

The Miracle of Unity consciousness transcends all fears
and overcomes all obstacles with a wondrous result:
an experience of pure love and freedom.

May you experience peace, love,
liberty and freedom in your life!

Prayer of Saint Francis

Lord, make me an instrument of your peace.
Where there is hatred, let me sow love.
Where there is injury, pardon,
Where there is doubt, faith.
Where there is despair, hope.
Where there is darkness, light.
Where there is sadness, joy.

Divine Master, grant that I may not seek
So much to be consoled as to console,
To be understood as to understand,
To be loved as to love.
For it is in giving that we receive,
In pardoning that we are pardoned,
And in dying that we are
born to eternal life.

About the Author

Kornelia Stephanie - Catalyst for Global Evolution in the 21st Century

Kornelia is respected as a leading-edge 'evolutionary' for personal transformation, leadership, and the birthing of the consciousness of the New Human. She is passionate about humanity's sovereignty, the authority over one's own life as empowered creation.

A multi-dimensional master, her journey has led her to walk intimately with her shadow, and in healing the wounds of the past she has embraced her divinity. Her deep understanding of the relationship between her physical body and that of the primary relationship with her Soul/Source is the foundation of what she teaches others: embodiment of the Divine in the physical.

Kornelia is an author, intuitive mystic, international speaker, a self-life mastery expert, an ascension guide, and, most importantly, a way-shower of transformation. Her works are about empowerment, self-love, and the unveiling of the truth for authentic living.

Kornelia specializes in 'Emotional Processing.' Recently, she created the 'Universal Wholeness Coaching Program' to help others establish their own coaching business, so that they could offer their gifts by coaching others into self-love. Kornelia regularly organizes and facilitates retreats in and near her home town of La Conner, WA. Check her website for her retreat and events schedule.

Kornelia's newest online creation, the 'What Is™ Game,' is an innovative catalyst to assist all to embody, through their own experiences, the consciousness of the living word. Speaking the world into being.

Her Divine Purpose is to lovingly engage others, in the most practical ways, in creating their daily living, *their lives*, in the New Earth.

To access her online membership and find out more about Kornelia and her work, visit her website at: www.korneliaStephanie.com

Stay Connected

At first people refuse to believe that a strange new thing can be done, then they begin to hope that it can be done, then they see it can be done, then it is done and all the world wonders why it was not done centuries ago.   -Frances Hodgson Burnett

The World's Best Empowerment Blueprint
Take the Quantum Leap as you soar into your new miraculous life with ease and grace. While relaxing at home, go deeper and release the victim. Reclaim your power and your birthright. Learn how to live an empowered life and actualize your Wealth Revolution. Bonus of the course: you will change your relationship to money.

$197.00

Live Your Heaven - Not Someone Else's
Be the Conscious Gardener tending to your own inner garden. Peace is an inside job. Seed your Peace and Gratitude Garden with you daily love, abundance and appreciation. IT'S YOUR HEAVEN. Guided Meditations with Audio support.

$27.00

Manifesting Miracles Now - Live Your Heaven
Expect miracles in your relationships, your health, your purpose, your finances, and more. Join our global miracle circle and learn how to manifest miracles in your everyday life. The explosion of miracles is everywhere. Self Love bonus series included with audio support.

$33.00

Keynote Speaker
Kornelia shares her messages with a worldwide audience in an electrifying way. As a member of the WSA (www.womenspeakerassociation.com) she will create a special, energetic talk designed for

non-profits, corporate and employee leadership, fundraising, spiritual events, and banquets. Topics include peace, emotional wealth, leadership, empowerment, and our personal and collective responsibility.

Personal Coaching/Private Retreats

I help people work with their shadow and release outdated beliefs, patterns, and habits that keep them stuck. My specialty is emotional processing, healing the core wounds of the personal pain in our lives so that we can step into the truth of our being and come home to self-realization.

Wholeness Coaching Certification Classes

Empower Others Wholeness Coaching Certification. Are you ready to take the next step and share your gifts with others? Become an empowerment success coach.

Private Network. Membership by Invitation only

Join our Happy New Earth Community, the "WE" generation of women and men who are leading in their self actualization. The New Earth Tribe, active and vital, meets regularly to inspire and be inspired. Daily inspirational messages for empowered living.

Next Step

You can access these wonderful links of support on my website at www.korneliastephanie.com. After ordering online, you may also claim your personal surprise gift from me by tearing our this page of the book, circle the items that you purchases, and send to me via snail mail at K. Dengel P.O. Box 119, La Conner, WA 98257-0119. Watch for your surprise!

Be sure to go to www.korneliastephanie.com and sign up for our newsletters to receive information on products to support YOU, the New Spiritual Human. Live a miraculous life!

~Kornelia